The Precious Garland
and
The Song of the
Four Mindfulnesses

THE WISDOM OF TIBET SERIES

By Tenzin Gyatso, The Fourteenth Dalai Lama

The Buddhism of Tibet
and
The Key to the Middle Way

volume 1

The Precious Garland and The Song of the Four Mindfulnesses

NAGARJUNA and
KAYSANG GYATSO
SEVENTH DALAI LAMA

Translated and edited by
Jeffrey Hopkins and Lati Rimpoche
with Anne Klein

FOREWORD BY HIS HOLINESS TENZIN GYATSO
THE FOURTEENTH DALAI LAMA

Harper & Row, Publishers
New York, Evanston, San Francisco, London

Library of Congress forms of authors' names:
Nāgārjuna;
Bskal-bzaṅ-rgya-mtsho, Dalai Lama VII, 1708–1757

FIRST U.S. EDITION

ISBN: 0-06-063541-X

LIBRARY OF CONGRESS CATALOG CARD NUMBER: 74-25688

75 76 77 78 79 10 9 8 7 6 5 4 3 2 1

Published under the aegis of the Library of Tibetan Works and Archives with the Authority of His Holiness the Dalai Lama as revealing oral tradition

Acknowledgements

The translators wish to thank Mr Gerald Yorke for many suggestions which improved the rendering in English.

Foreword

Sentient beings in general and mankind in particular have made and are continuing to make efforts to bring about their happiness and comfort by many different methods in accordance with their varying abilities. However, through a multitude of bad causes, both external and internal, they are continually tormented by many sufferings such as mental agitation and so forth. People in particular, unlike other living beings, create disturbances for themselves and others by reason of differences such as of country, race, political system and theory. As a result of these differences, groups of men are amassed, war is made and so on. Like intentionally putting a finger in its own eye, mankind consciously engages in many techniques that bring various undesirable consequences upon itself, such as causes for fear, man-made diseases, starvation and untimely death.

I have thought that under the circumstances of such a delicate time as described above, it would be wonderful if even a few people for a short period could have some internal peace. Also, many intelligent persons are analysing and seeking the meaning of emptiness. Based on that, I have commissioned the translation into English and publication of the following works:

> *The Buddhism of Tibet* and *The Key to the Middle Way*, both by myself.

> *The Precious Garland of Advice for the King*, by the protector Nāgārjuna. This good explanation is a great compendium of both the profound emptiness and the extensive deeds of compassion, illuminating as well techniques for social welfare.

The Song of the Four Mindfulnesses, by Kaysang Gyatso the Seventh Dalai Lama. This work has only a few words, but contains all the essentials of sūtra and tantra.

The present volume consists of the two texts by Nāgārjuna and Kaysang Gyatso. My two works are to be found in the first volume of this series.

The Buddhist monk, Tenzin Gyatso, BE 2516, AD 1972, the Tibetan Water Mouse year in the tenth month on the twelfth day.

Contents

Foreword   *page* 9

I   PRECIOUS GARLAND OF ADVICE FOR THE KING   13
    by Nāgārjuna

    Introduction   15

1   High Status and Definite Goodness   17

2   An Interwoven Explanation of Definite Goodness
    and High Status   32

3   The Collections for Enlightenment   47

4   Royal Policy   62

5   The Bodhisattva Deeds   78

Guide to the stanzas by Gyel-tsap   94

Notes   110

II SONG OF THE FOUR MINDFULNESSES   113
    by Kaysang Gyatso, the Seventh Dalai Lama

    Introduction   115

1   Mindfulness of the Teacher   117

2   Mindfulness of the Altruistic Aspiration to
    Highest Enlightenment   117

3   Mindfulness of Your Body as a Divine Body   117

4   Mindfulness of the View of Emptiness   118

Notes   119

I

The Precious Garland of Advice for the King

(Sanskrit: Rājaparikathā-ratnamālā)

NĀGĀRJUNA

Obeisance of the translators from Sanskrit into Tibetan
Homage to all Buddhas and Bodhisattvas

Introduction

Nāgārjuna was an Indian pandit from Vidarbha in south India who lived approximately four hundred years after Buddha's death. At that time the Mahāyāna teaching had diminished, and Nāgārjuna assumed the task of reviving it by founding the Mādhyamika school of tenets. Here, in his *Precious Garland*, he clarifies the Buddha's exposition of emptiness based on the *Perfection of Wisdom Sūtras* (*Prajñāpāramitā*). He presents the ten Bodhisattva stages leading to Buddhahood based on the *Sūtra on the Ten Stages* (*Daśabhūmika*). He details a Bodhisattva's collections of merit and wisdom based on the *Sūtra Set Forth by Akṣayamati* (*Akṣayamatinirdeśa*). The *Precious Garland* was intended primarily for the Indian king Śātavāhana, therefore, Nāgārjuna includes specific advice on ruling a kingdom. (The section on the undesirability of the body is written with reference to the female body simply because the king was a male. As Nāgārjuna says, the advice should be taken as applying to both males and females.) Among his works, the *Precious Garland* is renowned for extensively describing both the profound emptinesses and the extensive Bodhisattva deeds of compassion.

The translation is based on an oral transmission and explanation of the text received from His Holiness Tenzin Gyatso, the Fourteenth Dalai Lama, in Dharamsala, India in May of 1972. The text was translated in accordance with the commentary by Tsong-ka-pa's disciple Gyel-tsap (rGyal-tshab), whose guide has been included here to facilitate reading. The work was translated by Jeffrey Hopkins, who orally re-translated the English into Tibetan for verification and correction by Lati Rimpoche and then worked with Anne Klein to improve the presentation in English.

Chapter One

High Status and Definite Goodness

1 I bow down to the all-knowing,
Freed from all defects,
Adorned with all virtues,
The sole friend of all beings.

2 O King, I will explain practices solely
Virtuous to generate in you the doctrine,
For the practices will be established
In a vessel of the excellent doctrine.

3 In one who first practises high status
Definite goodness arises later,
For having attained high status one comes
Gradually to definite goodness.

4 High status is thought of as happiness,
Definite goodness as liberation,
The quintessence of their means
Are briefly faith and wisdom.

5 Through faith one relies on the practices,
Through wisdom one truly knows,
Of these two wisdom is the chief,
Faith is its prerequisite.

6 He who does not neglect the practices
   Through desire, hatred, fear or ignorance
   Is known as one of faith, a superior
   Vessel for definite goodness.

7 Having thoroughly analysed
   All deeds of body, speech and mind,
   He who realises what benefits self
   And others and who always practises is wise.

8 Not killing, no longer stealing,
   Forsaking the wives of others,
   Refraining completely from false,
   Divisive, harsh and senseless speech,

9 Forsaking covetousness, harmful
   Intent and the views of Nihilists—
   These are the ten white paths of
   Action, their opposites are black.

10 Not drinking intoxicants, a good livelihood,
   Non-harming, considerate giving, honouring
   The honourable, and love—
   Practice in brief is that.

11 Practice does not mean to
   Mortify the body,
   For one has not ceased to injure
   Others and is not helping them.

12 He who does not esteem the great path of excellent
   Doctrine which is bright with ethics, giving and patience,
   Afflicts his body, takes
   Bad paths like jungle trails;

13 His body entangled with vicious
    Afflictions, he enters for a long time
    The dreadful jungle of cyclic existence
    Among the trees of endless beings.

14 A short life comes through killing,
    Much suffering through harming,
    Through stealing poor resources,
    Through adultery enemies.

15 From lying arises slander,
    A parting of friends from divisiveness,
    From harshness hearing the unpleasant,
    From senselessness one's speech is not respected.

16 Covetousness destroys one's wishes,
    Harmful intent yields fright,
    Wrong views lead to bad views
    And drink to confusion of the mind.

17 Through not giving comes poverty,
    Through wrong livelihood, deception,
    Through arrogance a bad lineage,
    Through jealousy little beauty.

18 A bad colour comes through anger,
    Stupidity from not questioning
    The wise. The main fruit[1] of all this
    Is a bad migration for humans.

19 Opposite to the well known
    Fruits of these non-virtues
    Is a the arising of effects
    Caused by all the virtues.

20   Desire, hatred, ignorance and
     The actions they generate are non-virtues.
     Non-desire, non-hatred, non-ignorance
     And the actions they generate are virtues.

21   From non-virtues come all sufferings
     And likewise all bad migrations,
     From virtues all happy migrations
     And the pleasures of all births.

22   Desisting from all non-virtues
     And always engaging in virtues
     With body, speech and mind—these are
     Known as the three forms of practice.

23   Through these practices one is freed from becoming
     A hell-denizen, hungry ghost or animal;
     Reborn as a human or god one realises
     Extensive happiness, fortune and dominion.

24   Through the concentrations, immeasurables and form-
          lessnesses
     One experiences the bliss of Brahmā and so forth.
     Thus in brief are the practices
     For high status and their fruits.

25   The doctrines of definite goodness are
     Said by the Conquerors to be deep,
     Subtle and frightening to
     Children who are not learned.

26   'I am not, I will not be.
     I have not, I will not have',
     That frightens all children
     And kills fear in the wise.

27 By him who speaks only to help
Beings, it was said that they all
Have arisen from the conception of 'I'
And are enveloped with the conception of 'mine'.

28 'The "I" exists, the "mine" exists.'
These are wrong as ultimates,
For the two are not [established]
By a true and correct consciousness.

29 The mental and physical aggregates arise
From the conception of 'I' which is false in fact.[2]
How could what is grown
From a false seed be true?

30 Having thus seen the aggregates as untrue,
The conception of 'I' is abandoned
And due to this abandonment
The aggregates arise no more.

31 Just as it is said
That an image of one's face is seen
Depending on a mirror
But does not in fact exist [as a face],

32 So the conception of 'I' exists
Dependent on the aggregates,
But like the image of one's face
In reality the 'I' does not exist.

33 Just as without depending on a mirror
The image of one's face is not seen,
So too the 'I' does not exist
Without depending on the aggregates.

34   When the superior Ānanda had
      Attained [insight into] what this means,
      He won the eye of doctrine and taught it
      Continually to the monks.[3]

35   There is misconception of an 'I' as long
      As the aggregates are misconceived,
      When this conception of an 'I' exists,
      There is action which results in birth.

36   With these three pathways mutually causing each
      Other without a beginning, middle or an end,
      This wheel of cyclic existence
      Turns like the 'wheel' of a firebrand.

37   Because this wheel is not obtained from self, other
      Or from both, in the past, the present or the future,
      The conception of an 'I' ceases
      And thereby action and rebirth.

38   Thus one who sees how cause and effect
      Are produced and destroyed
      Does not regard the world
      As really existent or non-existent.

39   Thus one who has heard but does not examine
      The doctrine which destroys all suffering,
      And fears the fearless state
      Trembles due to ignorance.

40   That all these will not exist in nirvāṇa
      Does not frighten you [a Hīnayānist],
      Why does their non-existence
      Explained here cause you fright?

41   'In liberation there is no self and are no aggregates.'
If liberation is asserted thus,
Why is the removal here of the self
And of the aggregates not liked by you?

42   If nirvāṇa is not a non-thing,
Just how could it have thingness?
The extinction of the misconception
Of things and non-things is called nirvāṇa.

43   In brief the view of nihilism is
That actions bear no fruits; without
Merit and leading to a bad state,
It is regarded as the wrong view.

44   In brief the view of existence
Is that there are fruits of actions;
Meritorious and conducive to happy
Migrations, it is regarded as the right view.

45   Because 'is' and 'is not' are destroyed by wisdom,
There is a passage beyond merit and sin,
This, say the excellent, is liberation
From both bad and happy migrations.

46   Seeing production[4] as caused
One passes beyond non-existence,
Seeing cessation as caused
One no longer asserts existence.

47   Previously produced and simultaneously produced[5]
[Causes] are non-causes; thus there are no causes in fact,
Because [inherently existent] production is not
Conventionally or ultimately known at all.

48   When this is, that arises,
     Like short when there is tall.
     When this is produced, so is that,
     Like light from a flame.

49   When there is tall, there must be short,
     They exist not through their own nature,
     Just as without a flame
     Light too does not arise.[5a]

50   Having thus seen that effects arise
     From causes, one asserts what appears
     In the conventions of the world
     And does not accept nihilism.

51   He who refutes [inherently existent cause
     And effect] does not develop [the view of] existence,
     [Asserting] as true what does not arise from conventions;
     Thereby one not relying on duality is liberated.

52   A form seen from a distance
     Is seen clearly by those nearby.
     If a mirage were water, why
     Is water not seen by those nearby?

53   The way this world is seen
     As real by those afar
     Is not so seen by those nearby
     [For whom it is] signless like a mirage.

54   Just as a mirage is like water but is
     Not water and does not in fact exist [as water],
     So the aggregates are like a self but are
     Not selves and do not in fact exist [as selves].

55 Having thought a mirage to be
Water and then having gone there,
He would just be stupid to surmise
'That water does not exist.'

56 One who conceives of the mirage-like
World that it does or does not exist
Is consequently ignorant. When there is
Ignorance, one is not liberated.

57 A follower of non-existence suffers bad migrations,
But happy ones accrue to followers of existence;
One who knows what is correct and true does not rely
On dualism and so becomes liberated.

58 If through knowing what is correct and true
He does not assert existence and non-existence
And thereby [you think] he believes in non-existence,
Why should he not be a follower of existence?

59 If from refuting [inherent] existence
Non-existence then accrues to him,
Why from refuting non-existence
Would existence not accrue to him?

60 Those who rely on enlightenment
Have no nihilistic thesis,
Behaviour or thought, how can
They be seen as nihilists?

61 Ask the worldly ones, the Sāṃkhyas,
Owl-Followers[6] and Nirgranthas,
The proponents of a person and aggregates,
If they propound what passes beyond 'is' and 'is not'.

62   Thereby know that the ambrosia
Of the Buddhas' teaching is called profound,
An uncommon doctrine passing
Far beyond existence and non-existence.

63   Ultimately how could the world exist with a nature
Which has gone beyond the past, the present
And the future, not going when destroyed,
Not coming and not staying even for an instant?

64   Because in reality there is
No coming, going or staying,
What ultimate difference is there
Then between the world and nirvāṇa?

65   If there is no staying, there can be
No production and no cessation.
Then how could production, staying and
Cessation ultimately exist?[7]

66   How are things non-momentary
If they are always changing?
If they do not change, then how
In fact can they be altered?

67   Do they become momentary through
Partial or complete disintegration?
Because an inequality[8] is not apprehended,
This momentariness cannot be admitted.

68   When a thing ceases to exist through momentariness,
How can anything be old?
When a thing is non-momentary due to constancy
How can anything be old?

69 Since a moment ends it must have
    A beginning and a middle,
    This triple nature of a moment means
    That the world never abides for an instant.

70 Also the beginning, middle and end
    Are to be analysed like a moment;
    Therefore, beginning, middle and end
    Are not [produced] from self or other.

71 Due to having many parts 'one' does not exist,
    There is not anything which is without parts,
    Further without 'one' 'many' does not exist
    And without existence there is no non-existence.

72 If through destruction or an antidote
    An existent ceases to exist,
    How could there be destruction or
    An antidote without an existent?

73 Ultimately the world cannot
    Through nirvāṇa disappear.
    Asked whether it had an end
    The Conqueror was silent.

74 Because he did not teach this profound doctrine
    To worldly beings who were not receptacles,
    The all-knowing one is therefore known
    As omniscient by the wise.

75 Thus the doctrine of definite goodness
    Was taught by the perfect Buddhas,
    The seers of reality, as profound,
    Unapprehendable and baseless.[9]

76 Frightened by this baseless doctrine,
    Delighting in a base, not passing
    Beyond existence and non-existence,
    Unintelligent beings ruin themselves.

77 Afraid of the fearless abode,
    Ruined, they ruin others.
    O King, act in such a way
    That the ruined do not ruin you.

78 O King, lest you be ruined
    I will explain through the scriptures
    The mode of the supramundane,
    The reality that relies not on dualism.

79 This profundity which liberates
    And is beyond both sin and virtue
    Has not been tasted by those who fear the baseless,
    The others, the Forders[10] and even by ourselves.

80 A person is not earth, not water,
    Not fire, not wind, not space,
    Not consciousness and not all of them;
    What person is there other than these?

81 Just as the person is not an ultimate
    But a composite of six constituents,
    So too each of them in turn is a
    Composite and not an ultimate.

82 The aggregates are not the self, they are not in it,
    It is not in them, without them it is not,
    It is not mixed with the aggregates like fire and fuel,[11]
    Therefore how can the self exist?

83 The three elements[12] are not earth, they are not in it,
It is not in them, without them it is not;
Since this applies to each,
They like the self are false.

84 By themselves earth, water, fire and wind
Do not inherently exist;
When any three are absent, there cannot be one,
When one is absent, so too are the three.

85 If when three are absent, the one does not exist
And if when one is absent, the three do not exist,
Then each itself does not exist;
How can they produce a composite?

86 Otherwise if each itself exists,
Why without fuel is there no fire?
Likewise why is there no water, wind or earth
Without motility, hardness or cohesion?

87 If [it is answered that] fire is well known [not to exist
Without fuel but the other three elements exist
Independently], how could your three exist in themselves
Without the others? It is impossible for the three
Not to accord with dependent-arising.

88 How can those existing by themselves
Be mutually dependent?
How can those which exist not by themselves
Be mutually dependent?

89 If as individuals they do not exist,
But where there is one, the other three are there,
Then if unmixed, they are not in one place,
And if mixed, they cease to be individuals.

90   The elements do not themselves exist individually,
So how could their own individual characters do so?
What do not themselves individually exist cannot pre-
    dominate;[13]
Their characters are regarded as conventionalities.

91   This mode of refutation is also to be applied
To colours, odours, tastes and objects of touch,
Eye, consciousness and form,
Ignorance, action and birth,

92   Agent, object, acting and number,
Possession, cause, effect and time,
Short and long and so forth,
Name and name-bearer as well.

93   Earth, water, fire and wind,
Tall and short, subtle and coarse
Virtue and so forth are said by the Subduer
To cease in the consciousness [of reality].

94   The spheres of earth, water, fire
And wind do not appear to that
Undemonstrable consciousness,
Complete lord over the limitless.

95   Here tall and short, subtle and coarse,
Virtue and non-virtue
And here names and forms
All cease to be.

96   What was not known is known
To consciousness as [the reality of] all
That appeared before. Thereby these phenomena
Later cease to be in consciousness.

97 All these phenomena related to beings
    Are seen as fuel for the fire of consciousness,
    They are consumed through being burned
    By the light of true discrimination.

98 The reality is later ascertained
    Of what was formerly imputed by ignorance;
    When a thing is not found,
    How can there be a non-thing?

99 Because the phenomena of forms are
    Only names, space too is only a name;
    Without the elements how could forms exist?
    Therefore even 'name-only' does not exist.

100 Feelings, discriminations, factors of composition
     And consciousnesses are to be considered
     Like the elements and the self, thereby
     The six constituents[14] are selfless.

Chapter Two

An Interwoven Explanation of Definite Goodness and High Status

101   Just as there is nothing when
      A banana tree with all its parts
      Is torn apart, it is the same when a person
      Is divided into the [six] constituents.[15]

102   Therefore the Conquerors said,
      'All phenomena are selfless.'
      Since this is so, you must accept
      All six constituents as selfless.

103   Thus neither self nor non-self
      Are understood as real,
      Therefore the Great Subduer rejected
      The views of self and non-self.

104   Sights, sounds and so forth were said by the Subduer
      Neither to be true nor false;
      If from one position its opposite arises,
      Both in fact do not exist.[16]

105   Thus ultimately this world
      Is beyond truth and falsehood,
      Therefore he does not assert
      That it really is or is not.

106   [Knowing that] these in all ways do not exist,
How could the All-Knower say
They have limits or no limits,
Or have both or neither?

107   'Innumerable Buddhas have come, will come and are
Here at present; there are tens of millions of sentient
Beings, but the Buddhas will abide
In the past, the present and the future;

108   'The extinguishing of the world in the three
Times does not cause it to increase,[17]
Then why was the All-Knower silent
About the limits of the world?'

109   That which is secret for a common
Being is the profound doctrine,
The illusory nature of the world,
The ambrosia of the Buddha's teaching.

110   Just as the production and disintegration
Of an illusory elephant are seen,
But the production and disintegration
Do not really exist,

111   So the production and disintegration
Of the illusory world are seen,
But the production and disintegration
Ultimately do not exist.

112   Just as an illusory elephant,
But a bewildering of consciousness,
Comes not from anywhere,
Goes not, nor really stays,

113 So this world of illusion,
A bewildering of consciousness,
Comes not from anywhere,
Goes not, nor really stays.

114 Thus it has a nature beyond time;
Other than as a convention
What world is there in fact
Which would be 'is' or 'is not'?

115 This was why the Buddha
At all times kept silent
About the fourfold format: with or
Without a limit, both or neither.[18]

116 When the body, which is unclean,
Coarse, an object of the senses,
Does not stay in the mind [as unclean],
Although it is all the time in view,

117 Then how could this doctrine
Which is most subtle, profound,
Baseless and not manifest,
Appear with ease to the mind?

118 Realising that this doctrine is too
Profound and hard to understand,
The Buddha, the Subduer,
Turned away from teaching it.

119 This doctrine wrongly understood
Ruins the unwise,[19] because
They sink into the filth
Of nihilistic views.

120 Further, the stupid who fancy
Themselves wise,[20] having a nature
Ruined by rejecting [emptiness] fall headfirst
To a fearful hell from their wrong understanding.

121 Just as one comes to ruin
Through wrong eating and obtains
Long life, freedom from disease,
Strength and pleasure through right eating,

122 So one comes to ruin
Through wrong understanding
But gains bliss and complete enlightenment
Through right understanding.

123 Therefore having forsaken all nihilistic
Views and rejections concerning emptiness,
Strive your best to understand correctly
For the sake of achieving all your aims.

124 If this doctrine is not truly understood,
The conception of an 'I' prevails,
Hence come virtuous and non-virtuous actions
Which give rise to good and bad rebirths.

125 So long then as the doctrine that destroys
The misconception of an 'I' is not known,
Take care always to practise
Giving, ethics and patience.

126 A king who performs actions
With their prior, intermediary
And final practices
Is not harmed here or in the future.

127 Here through the practices come fame and happiness,
There is no fear now or at the point of death,
In the next life flourishes happiness,
Therefore always observe the practices.

128 The practices are the best policy,
It is through them that the world is pleased;
Neither here nor in the future is one
Cheated by a world that has been pleased.

129 The world is displeased
By the policies of non-practice;
Due to the displeasure of the world
One is not pleased here or in the future.

130 How could those of bad understanding
On a path to bad migrations, wretched,
Intent on deceiving others, having
Wrong aims, understand what is meaningful?

131 How could one intent on deceiving
Others be a man of policy?
Through it he will be cheated
In many thousands of births.

132 One who seeks disfavour for an enemy
Should neglect his faults and observe his virtues,
That brings help to oneself
And disfavour to the foe.

133 You should cause the religious
And the worldly to assemble
Through giving, speaking pleasantly,
Behaving with purpose and concordance.[21]

134 Just as by themselves the true words
Of kings generate firm trust,
So their false words are the best means
To create distrust.

135 What is not deceitful is the truth
And not a fabrication of the mind,
What to others is solely helpful is the truth,
The opposite is falsehood since it does not help.

136 Just as one splendid charity
Conceals the faults of kings,
So avarice destroys
All their wealth.

137 In peace there is profundity
From which the highest respect arises,
From respect come power and command,
Therefore observe peace.

138 From wisdom comes a mind unshakeable,
Relying not on others, firm
And not deceived, therefore,
O King, be intent on wisdom.

139 A lord of men having the four goodnesses,
Truth, giving, peace and wisdom,
Is praised by gods and men
As are the four good practices themselves.

140 Wisdom and practice always grow
For one who keeps company
With those whose speech is beneficial, who are pure,
Wise, compassionate and not contaminated.

141 Rare are helpful speakers,
Listeners are rarer,
But rarer still are words
Which though unpleasant help at once.

142 Therefore having realised the unpleasant
As being helpful, act on it quickly,
Just as when ill one takes nauseous
Medicine from one of a loving nature.

143 Always considering that life, health
And dominion are impermanent,
You will make an intense effort
Just to carry out the practices.

144 Seeing that death is certain, that
When dead one suffers from one's sins,
You should not sin, although
There might be passing pleasure.

145 Sometimes horror is seen
And sometimes it is not,[22]
If there is comfort in one,
Why fear you not the other?

146 Intoxicants lead to worldly scorn,
Affairs are ruined, wealth is wasted,
The unsuitable is done from delusion,
Therefore never take intoxicants.

147 Gambling causes avarice,
Unpleasantness, hatred, deception, cheating,
Wildness, lying, senseless and harsh speech,
Therefore never gamble.

148 Lust for a woman mostly comes
From thinking that her body is clean,
But there is nothing clean
In a woman's body.

149 The mouth is a vessel filled with foul
Saliva and filth between the teeth,
The nose with fluids, snot and mucus,
The eyes with their own filth and tears.

150 The body is a vessel filled
With excrement, urine, lungs and liver;
He whose vision is obscured and does not see
A woman thus, lusts for her body.

151 Just as some fools desire
An ornamented pot of filth,
So the ignorant and obscured
And the worldly desire women.

152 If the world is greatly attached
To the nauseous stinking body
Which should cause loss of attachment,
How can it be led to freedom from desire?

153 Just as pigs yearn greatly for
A source of excrement, urine and vomit,
So some lustful ones desire
A source of excrement, urine and vomit.

154 This filthy city of a body,
With protruding holes for the elements
Is called by stupid beings
An object of pleasure.

155   Once you have seen for yourself the filth
Of excrement, urine and so forth,
How could you be attracted
To a body so composed?

156   Why should you lust desirously for this
While recognising it as a filthy form
Produced by a seed whose essence is filth,
A mixture of blood and semen?

157   He who lies on the filthy mass
Covered by skin moistened with
Those fluids, merely lies
On top of a woman's bladder.

158   If whether beautiful or
Ugly, whether old or young,
All the bodies of women are filthy
From what attributes does your lust arise?

159   Just as it is not fit to desire
Filth although it have a good colour
And shape in its very freshness,
So is it with a woman's body.

160   How could the nature of this putrid corpse,
A rotten mass covered outside by skin,
Not be seen when it looks
So very horrible?

161   'The skin is not foul,
It is like a cloak.'
Over a mass of filth
How could it be clean?

162 A pot though beautiful outside
     Is reviled when filled with filth.
     Why is the body, when so filled
     And foul by nature, not reviled?

163 If against filth you revile,
     Why not against this body
     Which befouls clean scents,
     Garlands, food and drink?

164 Just as one's own or others'
     Filthiness is reviled,
     Why not revile against one's own
     And others' filthy bodies?

165 Since your own body is
     As filthy as a woman's,
     Should not you abandon
     Desire for self and other?

166 If you yourself wash this body
     Dripping from the nine wounds[23]
     And still do not think it filthy, what
     Use have you for profound instruction?

167 Whoever composes poetry with
     Metaphors which elevate this body—
     O how shameless! O how stupid!
     How embarrassing before the wise!

168 Since these sentient beings are obscured
     By the darkness of ignorance,
     They quarrel mostly over what they want
     Like dogs for the sake of some filth.

169   There is pleasure when a sore is scratched,
      But to be without sores is more pleasurable still;
      There are pleasures in worldly desires,
      But to be without desires is more pleasurable still.

170   If you thus analyse, even though
      You do not become free from desire,
      Because your desire has lessened
      You will no longer lust for women.

171   To hunt game is an endless
      Cause of a short life,
      Suffering and hell,
      Therefore always keep from killing.

172   Bad like a snake with poisonous
      Fangs, its body stained with filth,
      Is he who frightens embodied
      Beings when he encounters them.

173   Just as farmers are gladdened
      When a great rain-cloud gathers,
      So one who gladdens embodied beings
      When he encounters them is good.

174   Thus always observe the practices
      And not those counter to them.

      *   *   *   *   *   *

      If you and the world wish to gain
      The highest enlightenment,

175   Its roots are the altruistic aspiration
      To enlightenment firm like Meru, the king of mountains,
      The compassion which reaches to all quarters,
      The wisdom which relies not on duality.

176   O great King, listen to how
      Your body will be adorned
      With the two and thirty
      Signs of a great being.

177   Through the proper honouring of reliquaries,[24]
      Honourable beings, superiors and the elderly
      You will become a Universal Monarch,
      Your glorious hands and feet marked with [a design of]
        wheels.

178   O King, always maintain firmly
      What you have vowed about the practices,
      You will then become a Bodhisattva
      With feet that are very level.

179   Through gifts and pleasant speech,
      Purposeful and concordant behaviour
      You will have hands with glorious
      Fingers joined by webs [of light].

180   Through abundant giving
      Of the best food and drink
      Your glorious hands and feet will be soft;
      Your hands and feet and shoulder blades
      And the nape of your neck will broaden,
      So your body will be big and those seven areas broad.

181   Through never doing harm and freeing the condemned
      Beautiful will be your body, straight and large,
      Very tall with long fingers
      And broad backs of the heels.

182 Through promoting the vowed practices
Your good colour will be glorious,
Your ankles will not be prominent,
Your body hairs will grow upwards.

183 Through your zeal for knowledge and the arts
And so forth, and through imparting them
You will have the calves of an antelope,
A sharp mind and great wisdom.

184 If others seek your wealth and possessions,
Through the discipline of immediate giving
You will have broad hands, a pleasant complexion
And will become a leader of the world.

185 Through reconciling well
Friends who have been divided
Your glorious secret organ
Will retract inside.

186 Through giving good houses
And nice comfortable carpets
Your colour will be very soft
Like pure stainless gold.

187 Through giving the highest powers [or kingdoms]
And following a teacher properly
You will be adorned by each and every hair
And by a circle of hair between the eyebrows.

188 Through speech that is pleasant and pleasing
And by acting upon the good speech [of others]
You will have curving shoulders
And a lion-like upper body.

189 If you nurse and cure the sick,
Your chest will be broad,
You will live naturally
And all tastes will be the best.

190 Through initiating activities concordant
With the practices, the swelling on your crown[24a]
Will stand out well and [your body] will be
Symmetrical like a banyan tree.

191 Through speaking true and soft words
Over the years, O lord of men,
Your tongue will be long and
Your voice that of Brahmā.

192 Through speaking true words
Always at all times
You will have cheeks like a lion,
Be glorious and hard to best.

193 Through showing great respect, serving
Others and doing what should be done,
Your teeth will shine
Very white and even.

194 Through using true and non-divisive
Speech over a long time
You will have forty glorious teeth
Set evenly and good.

195 Through viewing things with love
And without desire, hatred or delusion
Your eyes will be bright and blue
With eyelashes like a bull.

196 Thus in brief know well
These two and thirty signs
Of a great lion of a being
Together with their causes.

197 The eighty minor marks arise
From a concordant cause of love;
Fearing this text would be too long,
I will not, O King, explain them.

198 All Universal Emperors
Are regarded as having these,
But their purity, their lustre and beauty
Cannot begin to match those of a Buddha.

199 The good major and minor marks
Of a Universal Emperor
Are said to arise from a single act
Of faith in the King of Subduers.

200 But such virtue accumulated with a mind
One-pointed for a hundred times ten million aeons
Cannot produce even one
Of the hair-pores of a Buddha.
Just as the brilliance of suns
Is slightly like that of fireflies,
So the signs of a Buddha are slightly like
Those of a Universal Emperor.

Chapter Three

The Collections for Enlightenment

201 Great King, hear how from the great
Scriptures of the Mahāyāna
The marks of a Buddha arise
From merit inconceivable.

202 The merit which creates all Solitary
Realisers, Learners and Non-Learners
And all the merit of the transient world
Is measureless like the universe itself.

203 Through such merit ten times extended
One hair-pore of a Buddha is achieved;
All the hair-pores of a Buddha
Arise in just the same way.

204 Through multiplying by a hundred
The merit which produces
All the hair-pores of a Buddha
One auspicious minor mark is won.

205 O King, as much merit as is required
For one auspicious minor mark,
So much also is required
For each up to the eightieth.

206 Through multiplying by a hundred
     The collection of merit which achieves
     The eighty auspicious minor marks
     One major sign of a great being arises.

207 Through multiplying by a thousand
     The extensive merit which is the cause
     Of achieving the thirty minor signs
     The hair-treasure like a full moon arises.[25]

208 Through multiplying by a hundred thousand
     The merit for the hair-treasure
     A protector's crown-protrusion
     Is produced, imperceptible [as to size].

     [Through increasing by ten million times a hundred
     Thousand the merit for the crown-protrusion
     There comes the excellence which gives the euphony
     Of a Buddha's speech and its sixty qualities.][26]

209 Though such merit is measureless
     For brevity it is said to have a measure
     And all of it is said to be
     Ten times the merit of the world.

210 When the causes of even the Form Body
     Of a Buddha are immeasurable
     As the world, how then could the causes
     Of the Body of Truth be measured?

211 If the causes of all things are small
     But they produce extensive effects,
     The thought that the measureless causes of Buddhahood
     Have measurable effects must be eliminated.

212 The Form Body of a Buddha
     Arises from collected merit,
     The Body of Truth in brief, O King,
     Arises from collected wisdom.

213 Thus these two collections cause
     Buddhahood to be attained,
     So in brief always rely
     Upon merit and wisdom.

214 Do not be lazy about this [amassing]
     Of merit to achieve enlightenment
     Since reasoning and scripture
     Can restore one's spirits.

215 Just as in all directions
     Space, earth, water, fire and wind
     Are without limit, so suffering
     Sentient beings are limitless.

216 The Bodhisattvas through their compassion
     Lead these limitless sentient beings
     Out of suffering and establish
     Them definitely in Buddhahood.

217 Whether sleeping or not sleeping,
     After thoroughly assuming [such compassion]
     He who remains steadfast,
     Even though he might become non-conscientious,

218 Always accumulates merit as limitless as all
     Sentient beings, for their number has no limit.
     Know then that since [the causes] are limitless
     Limitless Buddhahood is not hard to attain.

219 [A Bodhisattva] stays for a limitless time [in the world],
For limitless embodied beings he seeks
The limitless [qualities of] enlightenment
And performs virtuous actions without limit.

220 Though enlightenment is limitless,
How could he not attain it
With these four limitless collections
Without being delayed for long?

221 The limitless collections
Of merit and wisdom
Eradicate most quickly
The sufferings of mind and body.

222 The physical sufferings of bad migrations
Such as hunger and thirst arise from sins;
A Bodhisattva does not sin and through his merit
Does not [suffer physically] in other lives.

223 The mental sufferings of desire,
Fear, avarice and so forth arise
From obscuration; he knows them to be baseless
And so can uproot quickly [all mental suffering].

224 Since he is not greatly harmed
By physical and mental pain,
Why should he be discouraged even though
He leads the worldly beings in all worlds?

225 It is hard to bear suffering even for a little,
What need is there to speak of doing so for long?
What can ever harm a happy man
Who never suffers for an instant?

226   If his body does not suffer,
How can he suffer in his mind?
Through his great compassion he feels pain
For the world and so stays in it long.[27]

227   Do not then be lazy thinking
Buddhahood is far away.
Always strive hard for these collections
To wipe out faults and attain virtues.

228   Realising that ignorance, desire
And hatred are defects, forsake them completely.
Realise that non-desire, non-hatred and non-ignorance
Are virtues and so practise them with vigour.

229   Through desire one is reborn a hungry ghost,
Through hatred in a hell, through ignorance
Mostly as an animal; through stopping these
One becomes a god or a human being.

230   To eliminate all defects and maintain
The virtues are the practices of high status;
To wipe out all misconceptions through the conscious-
ness
[Of reality] is the practice of definite goodness.

231   With respect and without stint you should construct
Images of Buddha, reliquaries and temples
And provide abundant riches,
Food, necessities and so forth.

232   Please construct from all precious substances
Images of Buddha with fine proportions,
Well designed and sitting on lotuses
Adorned with all precious substances.

233 You should sustain with all endeavour
   The excellent doctrine and the assembly
   Of monks, and decorate reliquaries
   With gold and jewelled friezes.

234 Revere the reliquaries
   With gold and silver flowers,
   Diamonds, corals, pearls,
   Emeralds, cat's eye gems and sapphires.

235 To revere the teachers of the doctrine
   Is to do what pleases them,
   [Offering] goods and services
   And relying firmly on the doctrine.[28]

236 Listen to a teacher with homage
   And respect, serve and pray to him.
   Always respectfully revere
   The [other] Bodhisattvas.

237 You should not respect, revere
   Or do homage to others, the Forders,[29]
   Because through that the ignorant
   Would become enamoured of the faulty.

238 You should make donations of the word
   Of the King of Subduers and of the treatises
   He gave, as well as pages and books along
   With their prerequisites, the pens and ink.

239 As a way to increase wisdom
   Wherever there is a school
   Provide for the livelihood of teachers
   And bestow estates [for their provision].

240 In order to root out the suffering
     Of sentient beings, the old, young and infirm,
     You should establish through your influence
     Barbers and doctors in your kingdom.

241 Please act with good wisdom and provide
     Hostels, amusement centres, dikes,
     Ponds, rest-houses, water-vessels,
     Beds, food, grass and wood.

242 Please establish rest-houses
     In all temples, towns and cities
     And provide water-vessels
     On all arid roadways.

243 Always care compassionately for
     The sick, the unprotected, those stricken
     With suffering, the lowly and the poor
     And take special care to nourish them.

244 Until you have given to monks and beggars
     Seasonally appropriate food
     And drink, produce, grain and fruit,
     You should not partake of them.

245 At the sites of the water-vessels
     Place shoes, umbrellas, water-filters,
     Tweezers for removing
     Thorns, needles, thread and fans.

246 Within the vessels place the three medicinal
     Fruits, the three fever medicines, butter,
     Honey, salve for the eyes and antidotes
     To poison, written spells and prescriptions.[30]

247 At the sites of the vessels place
Salves for the body, feet and head,
Wool, small chairs, gruel, jars,
Pots, axes and so forth.

248 Please have small containers
In the shade filled with sesame,
Rice, grains, foods, molasses
And suitable water.

249 At the openings of ant-hills
Please have trustworthy men
Always put food and water,
Sugar and piles of grain.

250 Before and after taking food
Offer appropriate fare
To hungry ghosts, dogs,
Ants, birds and so forth.

251 Provide extensive care
For the persecuted, the victims [of disasters],
The stricken and diseased,
And for the worldly beings in conquered areas.

252 Provide stricken farmers
With seeds and sustenance,
Eliminate high taxes
By reducing their rate.

253 Protect [the poor] from the pain of wanting [your
wealth],
Set up no [new] tolls and reduce those [that are heavy],
Free them from the suffering [that follows when
The tax collector] is waiting at the door.

254 Eliminate thieves and robbers
In your own and others' countries.
Please set prices fairly and keep
Profits level [when things are scarce].

255 You should know full well [the counsel]
That your ministers have offered,
And should always follow it
If it benefits the world.

256 Just as you love to think
What could be done to help yourself,
So should you love to think
What could be done to help others.

257 If only for a moment make yourself
Available for the use of others
Just as earth, water, fire, wind, medicine
And forests [are available to all].

258 Even during the time needed to take seven steps
Merit measureless as the sky
Is produced in Bodhisattvas
Who are well disposed to giving wealth away.

259 If you give to the needy
Girls of beauty well adorned,
You will thereby master the spells
To retain the excellent doctrine.

260 Formerly the Subduer provided
Along with every need and so forth
Eighty thousand girls
With all adornments.

261 Lovingly give to beggars
Various and glittering
Clothes, ornaments, perfumes,
Garlands and enjoyments.

262 If you provide [facilities]
For those most deprived who lack
The means [to study] the doctrine,
There is no greater gift than that.

263 Even give poison to
Those whom it will help,
But do not give the best food
To those whom it will not help.

264 Just as some say that it will help
A cut finger to hold a snake,
So it is said that the Subduer
Brings discomfort to help others.

265 You should respect most highly
The excellent doctrine and its teachers,
You should listen reverently to it
And then give it to others.

266 Take no pleasure in worldly talk, but take
Delight in what passes beyond the world,
Cause good qualities to generate in others
In the same way that you wish them for yourself.

267 Please be not satisfied with the doctrines you have
Heard, but retain the meanings and discriminate.
Please always make great effort
To offer teachers presents.

268 Recite not from the worldly Nihilists,
Stop debating in the interests of pride,
Praise not your own good qualities,
But stress those even of your foes.

269 Do not say what hurts,
With evil intent talk
Not of others, analyse
Your own mistakes yourself.

270 You should free yourself completely from
The faults the wise decry in others,
And through your power cause
Others to do the same.

271 Consider the harm done to you by others
As created by your former deeds, be not angry,
Act in such a way that you do not cause
More suffering and your own faults will disappear.

272 Provide help to others
Without hope of reward,
Bear suffering alone and
Share your pleasures with beggars.

273 Do not be inflated even when you have acquired
The prosperity of gods.
Do not even be depressed
By the disadvantageous poverty of hungry ghosts.

274 For your own sake always speak the truth.
Even should it cause your death
Or ruin your kingdom,
Do not speak in any other way.

275 Always observe the discipline
Of actions as it has been explained,
Then, O glorious one, you will become
The best of models upon earth.

276 You should always well analyse
Everything before you act,
Through seeing things just as they are
You will not rely on others.

277 Through these practices your kingdom will be happy,
A broad canopy of fame
Will rise in all directions,
And your ministers will revere you completely.

278 The causes of death are many,
Those of staying alive are few,
These too can become the causes of death,
Therefore always perform the practices.

279 If you carry out the practices,
The mental happiness which arises
In the world and yourself
Is most beneficial.

280 Through the practices you will
Sleep and awaken in happiness;
Faultless in your inner nature
Happy will even be your dreams.

281 Intent on serving your parents, respectful
To the principals of your lineage,
Using your resources well, patient, generous,
With kindly speech, without divisiveness and truthful,

282   Through performing such discipline for one
      Lifetime you will become a king of gods;
      As such you will do still more,
      Therefore observe such practices.

283   Even three times a day to offer
      Three hundred cooking pots of food
      Does not match a portion of the merit
      Acquired in one instant of love.

284   Though [through love] you are not liberated
      You will attain the eight virtues of love,
      Gods and humans will be friendly,
      Even [non-humans] will protect you,

285   You will have pleasures of the mind and many
      [Of the body], poison and weapons will not harm you,
      Effortlessly will you attain your aims
      And be reborn in the world of Brahmā.

286   If you cause sentient beings to generate
      The aspiration to enlightenment and make it firm,
      Your own aspiration will always be
      To enlightenment firm like [Meru] king of mountains.

287   Through faith you will not be without leisure,
      Through good ethics you will have good migrations,
      Through becoming familiar with emptiness
      You will be unattached to all phenomena.

288   Through not wavering you will attain awareness,
      And intelligence through thinking; through respect
      You will realise what the doctrines mean,
      Through their retention you will become wise.

289 Through not causing the hearing and the giving
Of the doctrine to be obscured
You will company with Buddhas
And will quickly attain your wish.

290 Through non-attachment you will learn what [the doc-
trines] mean,
Through not being miserly your resources will increase,
Through not being proud you will become chief [of
those respected],
Through enduring the doctrine you will attain retention.

291 Through giving the five essentials[31]
As well as non-fright to the frightened
No evil will there be to harm you,
Of the mighty you will be the best.

292 Through offering many lamps
At reliquaries and elsewhere
And oil for lamps in dark places
Your divine eye will open.

293 Through offering bells and instruments
For the worship of reliquaries
And elsewhere drums and trumpets,
Your divine ear will open.

294 Through not relating others' mistakes
And not talking of their defective limbs,
But protecting their minds, you will gain
Knowledge of the minds of others.

295 Through giving conveyances and shoes,
    Through serving the feeble and through
    Providing teachers with youths you will acquire
    The skill to create magical emanations.[32]

296 Through acting to promote the doctrine,[33]
    Remembering its books and their meaning,
    And through stainless giving of the doctrine
    You will remember your continuum of lives.

297 Through knowing thoroughly, correctly and truly
    That no phenomena inherently exist,
    You will attain the sixth clairvoyance
    That extinguishes all contamination well.

298 Through cultivating the wisdom of reality which is
    The same [for all phenomena] and is moistened with
      compassion
    For the sake of liberating all sentient beings,
    You will become a Conqueror with all the excellences.

299 Through various pure aspirations
    Your Buddha Land will be purified,
    Through offering gems to the King
    Of Subduers you will give out infinite light.

300 Therefore knowing how actions
    And their effects agree,
    For your own sake help beings
    Always and so help yourself.

Chapter Four

Royal Policy

301 A king who does what is not righteous
And not suitable is mostly praised
By his subjects, for it is hard to know
What he will or will not tolerate;
Therefore it is hard to know
What is useful or not [to say].[34]

302 If useful but unpleasant words
Are hard to speak to someone else,
What could I, a monk, say to a king
Who is a lord of the great earth?

303 But because of my affection for you
And through my compassion for all beings,
I tell you without hesitation
That which is useful but unpleasant.

304 The Blessed One said that students are to be told
The truth, gentle, meaningful and salutary,
At the proper time and from compassion.
That is why you are being told all this.

305 O steadfast one, if true words
Are spoken without anger,
One should take them as fit to be
Heard, like water fit for bathing.

306 Realise that I am telling you
     What is useful here and later.
     Act on it so as to help
     Yourself and also others.

307 If you do not make contributions
     Of the wealth obtained from former giving,
     Through your ingratitude and attachment
     You will not obtain wealth in the future.

308 Here in the world workers do not carry
     Provisions for a journey unpaid.
     In the same way lowly beggars who carry [what you
         give them] multiplied
     A hundred times for your future life will not do so
         without payment.

309 Always be of exalted mind
     Delighting in exalted deeds,
     From exalted actions arise
     All effects that are exalted.

310 Create centres of doctrine, abodes
     Of the Three Jewels and fame
     And glory which lowly kings
     Have not even conceived in their minds.

311 O King, it is best not to create
     Centres of doctrine which do not stir
     The hairs of neighbouring kings because
     Of ill repute even after death.

312 Use even all your wealth to cause
The exalted to become free
From pride, and [the equal] to become delighted and to
   overcome
The inclinations of the lowly through your great
exaltation.[35]

313 Having let go of all possessions
[At death] powerless you must go elsewhere,
But all that has been used for the doctrine
Precedes you [as good karma].

314 All the possessions of a previous king
Come under the control of his successor
Of what use are they then to the former
King for practice, happiness or fame?

315 Through using wealth there is happiness here and now,
Through giving there is happiness in the future,
From wasting it without using it or giving it away,
There is only misery. How could there be happiness?

316 Because of lack of power while dying, you will be
Unable to give by way of your ministers,
Shamelessly they will lose affection
For you and will seek to please the new king.

317 Therefore while in good health create now
Centres of doctrine with all your wealth,
For you are living amidst the causes
Of death like a lamp standing in a breeze.

318 Also other centres of doctrine
Established by the previous king,
All the temples and so forth,
Should be sustained as before.

319 Please have them attended by those
Who harm not others, keep their vows,
Are virtuous, truthful, kind to visitors,
Patient, non-combative and always industrious.

320 Cause the blind, the sick, the lowly,
The protectorless, the wretched
And the crippled equally to attain
Food and drink without interruption.

321 Provide all types of support
For practitioners who do not seek it
And even for those living
In the realms of other kings.

322 At all centres of the doctrine
Appoint attendants who are
Energetic, without greed, skilful,
Religious and not harmful.

323 Appoint ministers who know good policy,
Who practise the doctrine, are affectionate,
Pure, friendly, undaunted, of good lineage,
Of excellent disposition and grateful.

324 Appoint generals who are generous,
Without attachments, brave, affectionate,
Who use [the king's wealth] properly, are steadfast,
Always attentive and practise the doctrine.

325 Appoint as administrators men who are old,
Of religious disposition, pure and able,
Who know what should be done, are well read, unbiased,
Affectionate and understand good policy.

326 Every month you should hear from them
About all the income and expenses
And having heard you should tell then all that should
Be done for the centres of doctrine and so forth.

327 If your kingdom exists for the doctrine
And not for fame or desire,
Then it will be extremely fruitful,
If not its fruit will be misfortune.

328 O lord of men, since in this world
Most are prone to deceive each other,
Listen to how your kingdom
And your practice should be.

329 Let there always be around you many men
Old in experience, of good lineage,
Who know what policy is good, shrink from sin,
Are agreeable and know what should be done.

330 Even if they rightfully have fined,
Bound or punished people and so forth,
You, being softened with compassion,
Should always take care [of the offenders].

331 O King, through compassion you should always
Generate an attitude of help
Even for all those embodied beings
Who have committed appalling sins.

332 Especially generate compassion
For those murderers, whose sins are horrible;
Those of fallen nature are receptacles
Of compassion from those whose nature is great.

333 Free the weaker prisoners
After a day or five days,
Do not think the others
Are never to be freed.

334 For each one whom you do not think
To free you will lose the layman's vow,
Because you will have lost the vow
Faults will constantly be amassed.

335 As long as the prisoners are not freed,
They should be made comfortable
With barbers, baths, food, drink,
Medicine and clothing.[36]

336 Just as unworthy sons are punished
Out of a wish to make them worthy,
So punishment should be enforced with compassion
And not through hatred or desire for wealth.

337 Once you have analysed the angry
Murderers and recognised them well,
You should banish them without
Killing or tormenting them.

338 In order to maintain control, oversee your country
Through the eyes of agents;
Attentive and mindful
Always do those things that accord with the practices.

339 Continually honour in an exalted way
     Those who are well grounded in good qualities
     With gifts, respect and reverence,
     And likewise honour all the rest.

340 The birds of the populace will alight upon
     The royal tree which provides the shade of patience,
     The flourishing flowers of respect
     And large fruits of resplendent giving.

341 A king whose nature is to give
     Is liked if he is strong,
     Like a sugared pastry
     Hardened with cardamom pepper.

342 If you analyse and reason thus
     Your dominion will not degenerate,
     It will not be without principle
     Nor become a system without rule.

343 You did not bring your kingdom with you from your
     Former life nor will you take it to the next,
     Since it was won by virtues, to act
     For it without virtue is wrong.

344 O King, exert yourself
     To avert a succession
     Of miserable supplies for the kingdom
     Through [misuse of] the royal resources.

345 O King, exert yourself
     To increase the succession
     Of the kingdom's resources
     Through [proper use of] your own.

346 Although a Universal Monarch rules
Over the four continents, his pleasures
Are regarded as only two,
The physical and the mental.

347 Physical feelings of pleasure
Are only a lessening of pain,
Mental pleasures are made by thought,
Created only by the intellect.

348 All the wealth of worldly pleasures
Are but a lessening of suffering,
Or are only [creations of] thought,
Thus they are in fact not real.

349 One by one there is enjoyment of
Continents, countries, towns and homes,
Conveyances, seats, clothing, beds, food,
Drink, elephants, horses and women.

350 When the mind has any [one of these
As its object] there is said to be
Pleasure, but if no attention is paid to the others,
The others are not then in fact real [causes of pleasure].

351 When [all] five senses, eye and so forth,
[Simultaneously] apprehend their objects,
A thought [of pleasure] does not refer [to all of them],
Therefore at that time they do not all give pleasure.

352 Whenever any of the [five] objects is known
[As pleasurable] by one of the [five] senses,
Then the remaining [objects] are not so known[37]
Since they are not real [causes of pleasure].

353   When the mind apprehends a past object
Which has been picked up by the senses,
It imagines and fancies
It to be pleasurable.

354   Also the one sense which here [in the world
Is said to] know one object,
Without an object is as unreal
As that object is without it.

355   Just as a child is said to be born
Dependent on a father and mother,
So a consciousness is said to arise
Dependent on a sense and on a form.

356   Past and future objects
And the senses are unreal,
So too are present [objects] since
They are not distinct from these two.[38]

357   Just as due to error the eye perceives
A [whirling] firebrand as a wheel,
So the senses apprehend
Present objects [as if real].

358   The senses and their objects are regarded
As being composed of the elements,
Since the individual elements
Are unreal, so too are those objects.

359   If each element is different
It follows that there could be fire without fuel,
If mixed they would be characterless[39]
And this is true of the other elements.

360   Because the elements are unreal in both
      These ways so too is composition,
      Because composition is unreal
      So too in fact are forms.

361   Also because consciousnesses, feelings,
      Discriminations and factors of composition each
      Are not self-existent realities in any way,
      [Pleasures] are not ultimately real.

362   Just as a lessening of pain
      Is fancied to be real pleasure,
      So a suppression of pleasure
      Is also fancied to be pain.

363   Thus attachment to finding pleasure
      And to separating from pain
      Are to be abandoned because they do not inherently
      Exist; thereby for those who see thus there is liberation.

364   What sees [reality]? Conventionally they say
      It is the mind, for without mental factors
      There can be no mind, and [a second mind],
      Because unreal, cannot be simultaneous.[40]

365   Knowing thus truly and correctly
      That animate beings are unreal,
      Not being subject [to rebirth] and without grasping, one
      Passes [from suffering] like a fire without its cause.

366   Bodhisattvas also who have seen it thus,
      Seek perfect enlightenment with certainty,
      They maintain a continuity of existence
      Until enlightenment only through their compassion.

367 The collections [of merit and wisdom] of Bodhisattvas
Were taught by the Tathāgata in the Mahāyāna,
Disliked by the bewildered
The Mahāyāna is derided.

368 Either through not knowing virtues and defects,
Or identifying the defective as virtuous,
Or through disliking virtues,
They deride the Mahāyāna.

369 He who despises the Mahāyāna,
Knowing that to harm others is wrong
But that to help them is virtuous,
Is called one who dislikes virtues.

370 He who despises Mahāyāna, the source
Of all virtues in that [it teaches] taking delight
Solely in the aims of others and not looking
To one's own, consequently burns himself.

371 One with faith [in emptiness forsakes it] through misconception,
Another who is angry [forsakes emptiness] through
disliking it;
If even the faithful one is said to be burned, what can be
said
About the one who is disinclined through despising it?

372 Just as it is explained in medicine
That poison can be driven out by poison,
What contradiction is there in saying that
The injurious can be driven out by suffering?

373   It is widely known that motivation
      Determines practices and that the mind
      Is most important. How then could even suffering not be
        helpful
      For one who gives assistance with the motivation to
        help others?

374   If even [in ordinary life] pain can bring future benefit,
      [Accepting suffering] beneficial for
      One's own and others' happiness of course will help;
      This practice from of old is known as the excellent
        method.

375   Through relinquishing small pleasures
      There is extensive happiness [later];
      Seeing the greater happiness, the resolute
      Should relinquish their small pleasures [now].

376   If such things cannot be borne,
      Then doctors giving pungent
      Medicines would disappear. It is not [reasonable]
      To forsake [great pleasure for the small].

377   Sometimes what is normally thought unhelpful
      Is regarded as beneficial by the wise;
      General rules and their exceptions
      Are highlighted in all treatises.

378   Who with intelligence would deride
      Deeds motivated by compassion
      And the stainless wisdom as explained
      In the Mahāyāna?

379 Due to the great extent and depth
Of the Mahāyāna, it is derided
Through ignorance by the untrained and lazy,
Who are the foes of themselves and others.

380 The Mahāyāna has a nature
Of giving, ethics, patience, effort,
Concentration, wisdom and compassion,
How could it ever explain things badly?

381 Others' aims are [achieved] through giving and ethics,
One's own are [achieved] through patience and effort,
Concentration and wisdom cause liberation,
These epitomise the sense of the Mahāyāna.

382 The aims of benefiting oneself and others and the
      meaning
Of liberation as briefly taught [in the Hīnayāna]
By Buddha are contained in the six perfections,
Therefore the Mahāyāna is the word of Buddha.

383 Those blind with ignorance cannot bear
The Mahāyāna where Buddha taught
The great path of enlightenment
Consisting of merit and wisdom.

384 A Conqueror is said to have attributes that cannot be
      conceived because
The attributes [which are his causes] are inconceivable
      like the sky,
Therefore let the great nature of a Buddha as
Explained in the Mahāyāna be accepted.

385 Even [Buddha's] ethics were beyond
The scope of Śāriputra, so why
Is the inconceivable great nature
Of a Buddha not accepted?

386 The teaching in the Mahāyāna of non-production
And of extinction in the Hīnayāna are the same
Emptiness [since they show that inherent existence] is
    extinguished
And that nothing [inherently existent] is produced;
Then let the Mahāyāna be accepted [as Buddha's word].

387 If emptiness and the great nature
Of a Buddha are viewed thus with reason,
How could what is taught in the two vehicles
Be of unequal value for the wise?[41]

388 What the Tathāgata taught with a special
Intention is not easy to understand.
Because he taught one as well as three vehicles
You should therefore protect yourself through indiffer-
    ence.[42]

389 There is no fault with indifference, but there is fault
From despising it; how then could there be virtue?
Therefore those who seek good for themselves
Should not despise the Mahāyāna.

390 Since all the aspirations, deeds and
Dedications of Bodhisattvas
Were not explained in the Hearers' vehicle, how then
Could one become a Bodhisattva through its path?

391 [In the Vehicle of the Hearers] Buddha did not explain
The bases for a Bodhisattva's enlightenment;
What greater authority for this
Is there than the Conqueror?

392 How could the fruit of Buddhahood be superior
[If achieved] through the path common to Hearers
Which has the bases [of the Hearer enlightenment], the
    meanings of
The four noble truths and the auxiliary aids to en-
lightenment?

393 The subjects based on the deeds of Bodhisattvas
Were not mentioned in the [Hīnayāna] sūtras,
But were explained in the Mahāyāna, thus the clear
Sighted should accept it [as the word of Buddha].

394 Just as a grammarian [first] makes
His students read the alphabet,
So Buddha taught his trainees
The doctrines which they could bear.

395 To some he taught doctrines
To discourage sinning,
To some, doctrines for achieving merit,
To others, doctrines based on duality.

396 To some he taught doctrines based on non-duality, to
    some
He taught what is profound and frightening to the
    fearful,
Having an essence of emptiness and compassion,
The means of achieving [the highest] enlightenment.

397 Therefore the wise should extinguish
Any hatred for the Mahāyāna
And generate especial faith
To achieve perfect enlightenment.

398 Through faith in the Mahāyāna
And through the practices explained therein
The highest enlightenment is attained
And along the way all pleasures.

399 At that time [when you are a king] you should inter-
nalise
Firmly the practices of giving, ethics and patience,
Which were especially taught for householders
And which have an essence of compassion.

400 However, if through the unrighteousness
Of the world it is hard to rule religiously,
Then it is right for you to become a monk
For the practice and grandeur [to which it leads].

Chapter Five
The Bodhisattva Deeds

401 Having become a monk you should train
First with energy [in ethics],
Then take up the discipline of individual emancipation,
Hear [the scriptures recited] frequently, and ascertain
   their meaning.

402 Then, knowing the small faults, forsake
The sources to be forsaken;
With effort you should realise
Fully the fifty-seven faults.

403 Anger is a disturbance of mind,
Enmity disturbs it further,
Concealment is a hiding of faults,
Resentment a clinging to faulty ways.

404 Dishonesty is extreme deception,
Dissimulation, crookedness of mind,
Jealousy is to be hurt by the good qualities
Of others; miserliness is a fear of giving.

405 To be unembarrassed and unashamed
Is insensibility to oneself and others,
Inflatedness leads to disrespect,
While evil effort is a pollution from anger.

406   Arrogance is haughtiness,
      Non-conscientiousness is to neglect
      Virtues, pride has seven forms
      Each of which I will explain.

407   Boasting that one is lower than the lowly,
      Or equal with the equal, or greater than
      Or equal to the lowly
      Is called the pride of selfhood.

408   Boasting that one is equal to those
      Who by some quality are better than oneself
      Is the pride of being superior. Thinking
      That one is higher than the extremely high,

409   Who fancy themselves to be superior,
      Is pride greater than pride;
      Like an abscess in a tumour
      It is very vicious.

410   Conceiving an 'I' through ignorance
      In the five empty [aggregates]
      Which are called the appropriation
      Is said to be the pride of thinking 'I'.

411   Thinking one has won fruits not yet
      Attained is pride of conceit.
      Praising oneself for faulty deeds
      Is known by the wise as wrongful pride.

412   Deriding oneself, thinking
      'I am senseless,' is called
      The pride of lowliness.
      Such briefly are the seven prides.

413 Hypocrisy is to control the senses
For the sake of goods and respect,
Flattery is to speak pleasant phrases
For the sake of goods and respect.

414 Indirect acquisition is to praise
The wealth of others so as to win it,
Artful acquisition is to deride
Others in order to acquire their goods.

415 Desiring to add profit to profit
Is to praise previous acquisitions,
Reciting faults is to repeat
The mistakes made by others.

416 Non-collectedness is selfish excitement
That is inconsiderate of others,
Clinging is the attachment of
The lazy to their bad possessions.

417 Making differences is discrimination
Obscured through desire, hatred or confusion,
Not looking into the mind is explained
As not applying it to anything.

418 One who through laziness loses respect and reverence
For those doing practices that are similar
Is a spiritual guide who follows not the ways
Of the Blessed One; he is regarded as bad.

419 Attachment is a small entanglement
Arising from desire,
When strong it is a great entanglement
Arising from desire.

420   Fondness is an attitude
Of clinging to one's own property,
Unsuitable fondness is attachment
To the property of others.

421   Irreligious lust is the libidinous praise
Of women who [in fact] are to be abandoned.
Hypocrisy is [to pretend] that one possesses
Good qualities which one lacks, while desiring sins.

422   Great desire is extreme greed gone beyond
The fortune of knowing satisfaction,
Desire for gain is wanting to be known
Always as having superior qualities.

423   Non-endurance is an inability to bear
Injury and suffering; impropriety
Is not to respect the activities
Of a spiritual guide or teacher.

424   Not heeding advice is not respecting
Counsel from those of similar practice.
Intention to meet with relatives
Is loving attachment to one's kindred.

425   Attachment to objects is to relate
Their qualities in order to acquire them.
Fancying immortality is to be
Unaffected by concern over death.

426   Intention endowed with making
[One's qualities] understood
Is the thought that due to the appearance of knowledge
And wealth others will take one as a guide.

427 Intention endowed with desire is a wish
     To help others motivated by desire.
     To be affected with harmful intent
     Implies that one wishes to harm others.

428 Dislike is a mind that is unsteady,
     Desiring union is a dirtied mind,
     Indifference is a body without
     Effort, a laziness of lassitude.

429 Being affected is the influence
     On body and colour by afflictions,
     Not wishing for food is explained
     As discomfort due to gorging.

430 A very weak mind is taught
     As timidity and fear,
     Longing for desires is to desire
     And seek after the five attributes.[43]

431 Harmful intent toward others arises
     From nine causes: having senseless qualms
     About oneself, one's friends and foes
     In the past, present and future.

432 Sluggishness is non-activity
     Due to a heavy mind and body,
     Sleep is slumber, excitement is a
     Lack of physical and mental peace.

433 Contrition is repentance for bad deeds
     Which arises afterwards from grief,
     Doubt is to be of two minds about
     The truths, the Three Jewels and so forth.

434 [Householder] Bodhisattvas abandon the above,
While those who keep a [monk's] vows strictly abandon
   more.
Freed from these defects
The virtues are easily observed.

435 Briefly the virtues observed
By Bodhisattvas are
Giving, ethics, patience, effort,
Concentration, wisdom, compassion and so forth.

436 Giving is to give away completely
All one's wealth, ethics is to help others,
Patience is to forsake anger,
Effort, to delight in virtues;

437 Concentration is unafflicted one-pointedness,
Wisdom is ascertainment of the meaning of the truths,
Compassion is a mind that savours only
Mercy and love for all sentient beings.

438 From giving there arises wealth, from ethics happiness,
From patience a good appearance, from [effort in]
   virtue
Brilliance, from concentration peace, from wisdom
Liberation, from compassion all aims are achieved.

439 From the simultaneous perfection
Of all those seven [virtues] is attained
The sphere of inconceivable wisdom
The protectorship of the world.

440   Just as the eight levels of Hearers
Are explained in their vehicle,
So are the ten Bodhisattva
Stages in the Mahāyāna.

441   The first of these is the Very Joyous
Since the Bodhisattva is rejoicing.
He forsakes the three entwinements[44] and is born
Into the lineage of the Tathāgatas.

442   Through the maturation of these qualities
The perfection of giving becomes supreme,
He vibrates a hundred worlds
And becomes a great lord of the world.

443   The second is called the Stainless
Because the ten [virtuous] actions
Of body, speech and mind are stainless
And he naturally abides in them.

444   Through the maturation of these qualities
The perfection of ethics becomes supreme,
He becomes a Universal Monarch helping beings,
Master of the glorious [four continents]
And of the seven precious substances.

445   The third stage is called the Shining because
The pacifying light of wisdom arises.
The concentrations and clairvoyances are generated,
While desire and hatred are extinguished completely.

446   Through the maturation of these qualities
He practises supremely the deeds of patience
And putting an end to desire completely
Becomes a great wise king of the gods.

447 The fourth is called the Radiant
Because the light of true wisdom arises
In which he cultivates supremely
The auxiliaries of enlightenment.

448 Through the maturation of these qualities he becomes
A king of the gods in [the heaven] Without Combat,[45]
He is skilled in quelling the arising of the view
That the transitory collection [is a real self].

449 The fifth is called the Extremely Difficult to Overcome
Since all evil ones find it extremely hard to conquer
    him;
He becomes skilled in knowing the subtle
Meanings of the noble truths and so forth.

450 Through the maturation of these qualities he becomes
A king of the gods abiding in the Joyous Heaven,[46]
He overcomes the sources of afflictions
And of the views of all Forders.

451 The sixth is called the Approaching because he is
Approaching the qualities of a Buddha;
Through familiarity with calm abiding and special
    insight
He attains cessation and is thus advanced [in wisdom].

452 Through the maturation of these qualities he becomes
A king of the gods [in the heaven] of Liking Emanation.[47]
Hearers cannot surpass him, he pacifies
Those with the pride of superiority.

453 The seventh is the Gone Afar because
The number [of his qualities] has increased,
Moment by moment he can enter
The equipoise of cessation.

454 Through the maturation of these qualities he becomes a
master
Of the gods [in the heaven] of Control over Others'
Emanations,[48]
He becomes a great leader of teachers for he knows
Direct realisation of the [four] noble truths.

455 The eighth is the Immovable, the youthful stage,
Through non-conceptuality he is immovable
And the spheres of his body, speech and mind's
Activities are inconceivable.

456 Through the maturation of these qualities
He becomes a Brahmā, master of a thousand worlds,
Foe Destroyers and Solitary Realisers and so forth
Cannot surpass him in establishing the meaning [of the
doctrines].

457 The ninth stage is called
Good Intelligence,
Like a regent he has attained correct individual
Realisation and therefore has good intelligence.

458 Through the maturation of these qualities
He becomes a Brahmā who is master of a million worlds,
Foe Destroyers and so forth cannot surpass him
In responding to questions in the thoughts of sentient
beings.

459 The tenth is the Cloud of Doctrine because
The rain of excellent doctrine falls,
The Bodhisattva is consecrated
With light by the Buddhas.

460 Through the maturation of these qualities
He becomes a master of the gods of Pure Abode,
He is a supreme great lord, master
Of the sphere of infinite wisdom.

461 Thus those ten stages are renowned
As the ten of Bodhisattvas.
The stage of Buddhahood is different,
Being in all ways inconceivable,

462 Its boundless extent is merely said
To encompass the ten powers;
Each of his powers is immeasurable too
Like [the limitless number] of all migrators.

463 The limitlessness of a Buddha's
[Qualities] is said to be like
That of space, earth, water, fire
And wind in all directions.

464 If the causes are [reduced] to a mere
[Measure] and not seen to be limitless,
One will not believe the limitlessness
[Of the qualities] of the Buddhas.

465 Therefore in the presence of an image
Or reliquary or something else
Say these twenty stanzas
Three times every day:

466 Going for refuge with all forms of respect
To the Buddhas, excellent Doctrine,
Supreme Community and Bodhisattvas,
I bow down to all that is worthy of honour.

467 From all sins I will turn away
And thoroughly maintain all virtues,
I will admire all the merits
Of all embodied beings.

468 With bowed head and clasped hands
I petition the perfect Buddhas
To turn the wheel of doctrine and remain
As long as beings transmigrate.

469 Through the merit of having done all this and through
The merit that I have done and that I will do
May all sentient beings aspire
To the highest enlightenment.

470 May all sentient beings have all the stainless
Powers, freedom from all conditions of non-leisure,
Freedom of action
And good livelihood.

471 May all embodied beings
Have jewels in their hands and may
All the limitless necessities of life remain
Unconsumed as long as there is cyclic existence.

472 May all beings always be
[Born] as superior humans,[49]
May all embodied beings have
Wisdom and the support [of ethics].

473　May embodied beings have a good complexion,
　　　Good physique, great beauty, a pleasant appearance,
　　　Freedom from disease,
　　　Power and long life.

474　May all be skilled in the means [to extinguish
　　　Suffering], and have liberation from it,
　　　Absorption in the Three Jewels,
　　　And the great wealth of Buddha's doctrine.

475　May they be adorned with love, compassion, joy,
　　　Even-mindedness [devoid of] the afflictions,
　　　Giving, ethics, patience, effort,
　　　Concentration and wisdom.

476　May they have the brilliant major and minor marks [of a
　　　　Buddha]
　　　From having finally completed the two collections [of
　　　　merit and wisdom]
　　　And may they cross without interruption
　　　The ten inconceivable stages.

477　May I also be adorned completely
　　　With those and all other good qualities,
　　　Be freed from all defects and possess
　　　Superior love for all sentient beings.

478　May I perfect all the virtues
　　　For which all embodied beings hope
　　　And may I always relieve
　　　The sufferings of all sentient beings.

479   May those beings in all worlds
Who are distressed through fear
Become entirely fearless
Through merely hearing my name.

480   Through seeing or thinking of me
Or only hearing my name may beings attain great joy,
Naturalness free from error,
Definiteness toward complete enlightenment,

481   And the five clairvoyances
Throughout their continuum of lives.
May I ever in all ways bring
Help and happiness to all sentient beings.

482   May I always without harm
Simultaneously stop
All beings in all worlds
Who wish to commit sins.

483   May I always be an object of enjoyment
For all sentient beings according to their wish
And without interference as are the earth,
Water, fire, wind, medicine and forests.

484   May I be as dear to sentient beings as their
Own life and may they be very dear to me,
May their sins fructify for me
And all my virtues for them.

485   As long as any sentient being
Anywhere has not been liberated,
May I remain [in the world] for his sake
Even though I have attained enlightenment.

486　If the merit of this prayer
　　Had form, it would never fit
　　Into worlds as numerous
　　As sand grains in the Ganges.

487　The Blessed One said so,
　　And the reasoning is this:
　　[The limitlessness of the merit of] wishing to help
　　　limitless realms
　　Of sentient beings is like [the limitlessness of those
　　　beings].

488　These practices which I have
　　Explained briefly to you
　　Should always be as dear
　　To you as your body.

489　He who feels a dearness for the practices
　　Has in fact a dearness for his body;
　　If dearness [for the body] helps it,
　　The practices will do just that.

490　Therefore, pay heed to the practices as you do to your-
　　　self,
　　Pay heed to achievement as you do to the practices,
　　Pay heed to wisdom as you do to achievement,
　　Pay heed to a wise man as you do to wisdom.

491　He who has qualms that [reliance] on one who has
　　Purity, love, intelligence and helpful
　　Appropriate speech would be bad for himself,
　　Causes his own interests to be destroyed.

492 The qualifications of spiritual
     Guides should be known in brief by you;
     If you are taught by those who know
     Contentment, have compassion, ethics

493 And the wisdom which can drive out your afflictions,
     You should know [how to rely on] and respect them.
     You will attain the supreme achievement
     By following this excellent system:

494 Speak the truth, speak gently to sentient beings,
     Say what is by nature pleasant,
     What is [beneficial], most difficult to find;
     Speak to a plan, not defaming;
     Speak independently and well.

495 Be well-disciplined, contained, generous,
     Brilliantly attentive, of peaceful mind,
     Not excitable, nor deceitful,
     Not procrastinating, but steadfast.

496 Be certain like the moon [when it is] full
     And radiant like the sun in autumn,
     Be deep like the ocean
     And firm like Mount Meru.

497 Freed from all defects, adorned
     With all the virtues, become
     The sustenance of all sentient
     Beings and be omniscient.

498 These doctrines were not taught
Merely to help kings,
But with the wish in any way
To help other sentient beings.

499 O King, for you it would be right
Each day to think of this advice
So that you and others may achieve
Complete and perfect enlightenment.

500 For the sake of enlightenment the diligent should always
apply
Themselves to ethics, patience, non-jealousy and non-
miserliness;
Always respect a superior teacher and help
Altruistically without hope [of reward] those bereft of
wealth,
Always remain with superior people, leaving
The non-superior and maintaining thoroughly the
doctrine.

Here ends the *Precious Garland of Advice for the King* by the
great teacher, the Superior, Nāgārjuna. It was [first] translated by the Indian Abbot Vidyākāraprabhā and the Tibetan
translator monk Pel-tsek (dPal-brtsegs). Consulting three
Sanskrit editions, the Indian abbot Śīkanakavarma and the
Tibetan monk Pa-tsap-nyi-ma-drak (Pa-tshab-nyi-ma-grags)
corrected mistranslations and other points which did not accord
with the particular thought of the Superior [Nāgārjuna] and
his 'son' [Āryadeva]. It was printed at the great publishing
house below [the Potala in Lhasa].

Guide to the Stanzas
by Gyel-tsap (rGyal-tshab)

		STANZA
I Introduction		1–2
A Obeisance to and praise of Buddha		1
B Promise to compose the book		2
II The actual book		3–487

Chapter One: Cause and effect of high status and definite goodness   3–100

	STANZA
1 Setting the scene	3–7
a Order of the two doctrines	3
b Identification of their causes and of them as effects	4
c Difference of main and secondary of the two causes	5
d Characteristics of a trainee who is a vessel	6–7
2 Actual explanation of the causes and effects of high status and definite goodness	8–100
a Cause and effect of high status	8–24
(1) Extensive exposition	8–24b
(a) Practices for high status	8–21
1′ Sixteen practices for high status	8–10
a′ Thirteen practices to be ceased	8–10b
1″ Ceasing the ten non-virtues	8–9
2″ Ceasing other improprieties	10ab
b′ Three practices to engage in	10bc
c′ Summation	10d
2′ Non-existence of those in other systems	11–13
a′ Harming self and others through entering a bad path	11
b′ Persons who go on bad paths	12
c′ Faults of entering a bad path	13
3′ Fruits of wrongly engaging in those practices	14–19
a′ Fruits which concord with non-virtuous causes, a short life, etc.	14–18b
b′ Fruits which are fructifications into a whole lifetime, bad migrations	18cd

                                                               STANZA
     c′ Arising of fruits of virtue, opposite from those   19
     4′ Virtuous and non-virtuous causes and effects   20–1
  (b) Modes of practice   22
  (c) Fruits of practice   23–4b
(2) Summation   24cd
  b Cause and effect of definite goodness   25–100
(1) How definite goodness is described in sūtra   25–77
  (a) Brief explanation of the Conqueror's description
     of definite goodness   25–7
     1′ How definite goodness is described   25
     2′ Generation and non-generation of fear for the
      profound meaning by the ignorant and the wise   26
     3′ The Teacher's saying that fear arises from the
      conception of a self   27
  (b) Extensive explanation of definite goodness   28–74
     1′ Proving the conceptions of 'I' and 'mine' to be
     false   28–34
      a′ Actual proof   28–9
      b′ Attainment of liberation through abandoning
       these conceptions   30
      c′ Teaching reality through the example of a
       reflection   31–3
       1″ Example of ceasing sufferings and their
        sources through cognising the person and
        aggregates as not truly existing   31–2
       2″ The opposite example   33
      d′ Realisation of emptiness as the cause of liberation   34
     2′ Refutation of inherently existent bondage and
     liberation   35–45
      a′ Order of entry into cyclic existence   35–6
       1″ Identifying the root of cyclic existence   35
       2″ Example of cyclic existence   36
      b′ Order of ceasing cyclic existence   37–8
      c′ Benefits of realising emptiness   39
      d′ Nature of liberation   40–5
       1″ Unsuitability of fearing the extinguishment
        of the conception of a self at the time of
        the nirvāṇa without remainder   40
       2″ Liberation as the extinguishment of all
        conceptions of true existence   41–2

STANZA

       a″ Impossibility of an inherently existent
         non-thing as liberation   41
       b″ Impossibility of a thing as liberation   42ab
       c″ Meaning of liberation   42cd
     3″ Difference of wrong and right views   43–4
     4″ Liberation as the extinguishment of the
       conception of true existence even during
       the nirvāṇa with remainder   45
  3′ All phenomena as free of the extremes of per-
  manence and annihilation   46–74
    a′ Extensive exposition   46–56
      1″ Refuting inherently existent cause and
        effect   46–7
        a″ Cause and effect as free of the extremes
          of existence and non-existence   46
        b″ Refuting inherently existent cause and
          effect   47
      2″ Avoiding a contradiction with what is
        renowned in the world   48–9
      3″ Liberation through realising the meaning
        of non-duality   50–1
      4″ Illustrative example   52–6
        a″ Example of realising and not realising
          the reality of things   52–3
        b″ Refuting inherently existing aggregates   54
        c″ No liberation from cyclic existence if
          views of existence and non-existence
          are not abandoned   55–6
    b′ Absence of the fallacy of thereby falling to
    the view of annihilation   57–60
      1″ Necessity of cognising non-duality to
        attain liberation   57
      2″ Flinging the absurd consequence that a
        cogniser of what is free of the extremes
        has views of existence and non-existence   58–9
      3″ Absence of the fault of annihilation in
        realising the non-conceptual   60
    c′ Freedom from extremes as an uncommon
    feature of Buddhism   61–2
    d′ Refuting inherently existent things   63–74

			STANZA
	1″	Refuting inherently existent going and coming	63–4
	2″	Refuting inherently existent production, staying, and disintegration as characteristics of products	65
	3″	Tangentially refuting the assertions of non-Buddhists	66–8
		a″ Refuting the Vaiśeṣikas' assertion of permanent atoms	66–7
		b″ Refuting the Vaiśṇavas' assertion of a permanent person	68
	4″	Refuting inherently existent moments	69–74
		a″ All moments as having parts	69
		b″ Refuting inherent existence of what has parts	70
		c″ Refuting inherently existent things through the reason of their not being one or many	71–3b
		d″ Reason for not holding the world as having an end	73c–4
(c)	Summation		75–7
	1′ Conqueror's description of the profound		75
	2′ Faults of fearing it		76–7b
	3′ Exhorting the king to realise the profound		77cd
(2) Exhorting the king to learn the profound			78–100
(a) Setting the scene			78–9
(b) Two selflessnesses			80–100
	1′ Selflessness of persons		80–2
		a′ Unsuitability of the six constituents as the person	80–1
		b′ Refuting an inherently existent person through a fivefold analysis	82
	2′ Selflessness of other phenomena		83–100
		a′ Refuting an inherently existent form aggregate	83–99
			1″ Refuting inherently existent dependent-arisings	83–90
			a″ Their not being established as one or many	83
			b″ Therefore the elements are not inherently existent	84

	STANZA
c″ Non-inherent existence of composites	85–7
1: Contradiction of inherent existence and dependence of composites	85
2: Refuting an answer to that	86
3: Dispelling further debate	87
d″ Refuting proofs for inherent existence	88–90
2″ Refuting inherent existence of other forms	91ab
3″ Applying the refutation to other phenomena	91c–8
a″ Actual application	91c–2
b″ Sources for the emptiness of inherent existence	93–8
1: All phenomena as empty of inherent existence	93
2: Explanation	94–5
3: Stating proofs	96–7
4: No fault of falling to a view of annihilation	98
4″ Refuting inherently existent space	99
b′ Applying the refutation to the remaining aggregates	100

Chapter Two: Interwoven explanation of the cause and effect of definite goodness and high status | 101–200 |

1 Cause and effect of definite goodness	101–23
a Refuting extreme views	101–15
(1) Recalling the former explanation through another example	101
(2) Actual refutation of extreme views	102–14
(a) Non-inherent existence of self and selflessness	102–3
(b) Non-inherent existence of existents and non-existents	104–6
1′ Actual explanation	104–5
2′ Reason for not answering in any of the four extremes	106
(c) Dispelling an objection that not teaching an end to cyclic existence is wrong	107–14
1′ Objection	107–8

	STANZA
2' Answer	109–14
a' Example of the non-inherent existence of the world's production and cessation	109–11
1″ The profound as what is secret for non-receptacles	109
2″ Actual example	110–11
b' Example of the non-inherent existence of going and coming	112–13
c' Things are only nominally imputed	114
(3) Therefore, the four extremes were not taught	115
b Difficulty of cognising the profound	116–23
(1) Reason for the difficulty of cognising the profound	116–17
(2) Reason why Buddha did not explain the profound to non-receptacles	118
(3) Explaining that reason	119–23
(a) Faults of misconceiving the profound	119–20
(b) Example of the defects of misconception and the advantages of correct conception	121–2
(c) Advice to be conscientious about cognising the profound	123
2 Cause and effect of high status	124–74b
a Setting the scene	124–5
(1) Cycling in cyclic existence due to not cognising emptiness	124
(2) Advice to strive for high status as long as emptiness is not cognised	125
b Actual explanation of the cause and effect of high status	126–74b
(1) Achieving the causes for high status	126–43
(a) General exhortation to practise the causes for high status	126–32
1' Practising the causes which have five benefits	126–7
2' Practice is the best policy	128
3' Forsaking bad policies	129–32
a' Unsuitability of relying on bad treatises	129
b' Scorning reliance on bad treatises	130–1
c' Special policy for practice	132
(b) Training in the special causes for high status	133–43
1' Training in the four ways of assembling	133
2' Training in the four: speaking truth, etc.	134–9
a' The four individually	134–8

	STANZA
1″ Training in truth	134–5
2″ Training in giving	136
3″ Training in peace	137
4″ Training in wisdom	138
b′ Summation	139
3′ Relying on a special friend who is a cause for the increase of virtue	140–3
a′ Characteristics of a special friend	140
b′ Suitability of following him	141–2
c′ Continuously meditating on death or impermanence	143
(2) Forsaking the causes of bad migrations	144–73
(a) Brief explanation	144–5
(b) Extensive explanation	146–73
1′ Stopping attachment to intoxicants	146
2′ Stopping attachment to gambling	147
3′ Stopping attachment to women	148–70
a′ General refutation of the cleanliness of a woman's body	148
b′ Specific refutation of the cleanliness of a woman's body	149–69
1″ Refuting that a woman's parts are beautiful	149–54
a″ Unsuitability of attachment to a woman's body because of its only having a nature of filth	149–50
b″ Example	151
c″ Absence of the state of desirelessness if attached to a woman	152
d″ Though a woman's body is filthy, the stupid call it a cause of pleasure	153–4
2″ Refuting that the whole body is beautiful	155–68
a″ Stopping attachment to a woman's body in general	155–7
b″ Stopping attachment to its colour and shape	158–65b
1: Stopping attachment to the colour and shape of a woman's body in general	158

STANZA

        2: Stopping attachment to a beautiful
          body   159–63
          a: Unsuitability of attachment   159–61
          b: Suitability of disgust   162–3
        3: Thinking that one's own body,
          like a woman's, is filthy   164–5b
     c" Consequent unsuitability of attachment
        to a woman's body   165c–6
        d" Chiding persons who praise women   167–8
          3" Refuting that attachment to a woman is
        a cause of happiness   169
      c' Effect of meditating on filthiness   170
    4' Stopping hunting   171–3
       a' Forsaking killing   171
       b' Forsaking generating fear in others   172
       c' Generating pleasure in others   173
  (3) Summary: Abandoning non-practices and achieving
    the practices   174ab
3 Cause and effect of definite goodness   174c–200
  a Condensing the principal causes of highest enlightenment
    into three and training in them   174c–5
  b Training in the causes for achieving the thirty-two signs
    of a Buddha   176–96
  (1) Exhortation to listen   176
  (2) Actual explanation of the thirty-two marks of a
    Buddha   177–96
  c Reason for not elaborating here on the causes and effects
    of the minor marks   197
  d Difference between the marks of a Buddha and of a
    Universal Emperor   198–200
  (1) Difference in effects   198
  (2) Difference in causes   199–200d
  (3) Example   200efgh

*Chapter Three: Advice to train in the two collections which are
the causes of highest enlightenment*   201–300

1 Modes of the collections   201–11
  a Exhorting the king to listen   201

   b The limitlessness of the collection of merit   202–9

     (1) Actual explanation   202–8

        (a) Achieving one hair-pore of a Buddha through ten
             times the merit of Solitary Realisers, etc.   202–3

        (b) Achieving one minor mark of a Buddha through a
             hundred times the merit for achieving a hair-pore   204–5

        (c) Achieving one major mark of a Buddha through a
             hundred times the merit for producing all the
             minor marks   206

        (d) Achieving the circle of hairs on a Buddha's brow
             through a thousand times the merit for producing
             all the major marks   207

        (e) Achieving the crown protrusion through a thousand
             times the above merit   208

     (2) The collections are infinite but are taught to trainees
         as measureable   209

   c   The limitlessness of the collection of wisdom   210

   d   The limitlessness of the effects of the two collections   211

2   The effects of each collection   212–13

3   Advice not to be lazy about amassing the two collections   214–27

   a   Brief indication   214

   b   Extensive explanation   215–26

     (1) Advice not to be lazy about the collection of merit   215–20

        (a) Limitlessness of the merit of generating the
             aspiration to enlightenment   215–16

        (b) The ease of attaining Buddhahood through that
             cause   217–18

        (c) Ease of attaining Buddhahood by reason of
             having the four immeasurables   219–20

     (2) Advice not to be lazy about amassing the two
         collections   221–26

        (a) General teaching that through the two collections
             physical and mental suffering is removed   221

        (b) Removal of physical suffering by the collection of
             merit   222

        (c) Removal of mental suffering by the collection of
             wisdom   223

        (d) No cause for laziness about amassing the two
             collections   224–5

        (e) The power of great compassion   226

   c   Summation   227

	STANZA
4 The entities of the two collections	228–30
a Advice to forsake the opposites of merit and to rely on the meritorious	228
b The effects of the three poisons and of their opposites	229
c The actual two collections	230
5 Branches of the two collections	231–76
a Brief indication	231–9
(1) Branches of the collection of merit	231–7
(a) Establishing objects of worship	231–3
1′ Newly establishing objects of worship	231–2
2′ Worshipping them once established	233
(b) Worship	234–6
(c) Ceasing to worship unworthy objects	237
(2) Branches of the collection of wisdom	238–9
b Extensive exposition	240–76
(1) Branches of the collection of merit	240–64
(a) Giving one's own property	240–51
(b) Other giving	252–6
(c) Giving away all wealth	257–8
(d) Giving based on different needs	259–64
1′ Giving to humans with certain needs	259–60
2′ Giving to the needy	261
3′ Giving which accords with doctrine	262–4
(2) Branches of the collection of wisdom	265–76
6 Benefits arising to an amasser of merit	277–300
a Arising of five common good qualities	277–80
(1: 277a; 2: 277bc; 3: 277d–9; 4: 280ab; 5: 280cd)	
b Arising of twenty-five particular good qualities	281–300
(1: 281–2; 2: 283–5; 3: 286; 4: 287a; 5: 287b; 6: 287cd;	
7: 288a; 8: 288b; 9: 288c; 10: 288d; 11: 289; 12: 290a;	
13: 290b; 14: 290c; 15: 290d; 16: 291; 17: 292; 18: 293;	
19: 294; 20: 295; 21: 296; 22: 297; 23: 298; 24: 299ab;	
25: 299cd; summation 300)	
Chapter Four: Advice to train in flawless policy	301–400
1 Transition	301–6
a Because most do not dare to chide a king and praise him, it is fitting to listen to a good explanation	301–3

STANZA

b Instruction to listen to helpful words in accordance with
Buddha's advice ... 304
c Actual exhortation to listen to words helpful to oneself
and others ... 305–6

2 Extensive exposition of flawless royal policy ... 307–98
  a Royal policies ... 307–27
   (1) Increasing giving ... 307–8
   (2) Founding temples ... 309–17
    (a) Training in exalted thoughts and deeds ... 309
    (b) Achieving the four qualities ... 310
    (c) Special achievement ... 311–17
   (3) Maintaining what was established earlier ... 318–20
    (a) General teaching ... 318
    (b) Way of appointing caretakers ... 319
    (c) Equal maintenance ... 320
   (4) Providing even for those who do not seek it ... 321
   (5) Way of appointing ministers ... 322–7
    (a) Appointing religious leaders ... 322
    (b) Appointing ministers ... 323
    (c) Appointing generals ... 324
    (d) Appointing treasurers, etc. ... 325–7
  b Instruction in non-degeneration and development ... 328–45
   (1) Instruction in the non-degeneration of previously
existent practices ... 328–37
    (a) Transition ... 328
    (b) Actual instruction in non-degeneration ... 329–37
     1' Gathering those of special powers ... 329
     2' Making oneself compassionate ... 330–2
      a' Providing out of compassion ... 330
      b' Being compassionate especially to the sinful ... 331
      c' The correctness of the above ... 332
     3' Freeing prisoners and making prisons
comfortable ... 333–6
     4' If not reformable, banishing them from the
country ... 337
   (2) Developing previously non-existent practices ... 338–45
    (a) Achieving practices ... 338–42
     1' Sending out representatives ... 338–9
     2' Examples ... 340–2
    (b) Ceasing non-virtues ... 343–5

		STANZA
c	Achieving liberation and not forsaking the scriptures of the Mahāyāna	346–98
(1)	Training in the path of liberation	346–66
(a)	Refuting inherently existent objects of attachment, pleasant and painful feelings	346–64
1′	Refuting a real feeling of pleasure	346–61
a′	Transition	346–7
b′	Brief indication	348
c′	Extensive explanation	349–61
1″	Refuting proofs for real pleasure	349–60
a″	Refuting proofs for real mental pleasure	349–50
b″	Refuting proofs for real physical pleasure	351–60
1:	Refuting an aggregation of the five objects as a proof for real physical pleasure	351–3
2:	Refuting individual objects as proofs of real physical pleasure	354–60
a:	Actual refutation	354
b:	Refuting the proofs	355–60
1	Refuting inherently existing consciousnesses	355
2	Refuting inherently existing objects	356–7
3	Refuting inherently existing senses	358–60
a	Refuting inherently existing senses and objects through refuting inherently existing elements	358
b	Refuting inherently existing elements	359
c	Therefore, forms are not inherently existent	360
2″	Refuting the entity of real pleasure	361
2′	Refuting inherently existing pain	362
3′	Result of the refutation	363–4
a′	Liberation through realising emptiness	363
b′	Identifying the mind cognising emptiness	364

STANZA

    (b) Both Hīnayānists and Mahāyānists equally cognise
       the subtle emptiness   365–6
       1′ Necessity of cognising the subtle emptiness even
         to attain liberation   365
       2′ Difference between the Hīnayāna and Mahāyāna   366
  (2) Stopping the forsaking of the scriptures of the
Mahāyāna   367–98
    (a) Extensive exposition   367–96
       1′ Reason for the unsuitability of forsaking the
        scriptures of the Mahāyāna   367–79
        a′ Faults of deriding the Mahāyāna   367–71
          1″ Way the Mahāyāna is derided   367
          2″ Reasons for the derision   368–9
          3″ Faults of deriding the Mahāyāna   370–1
        b′ Therefore, the unsuitability of despising the
         Mahāyāna   372–9
          1″ Elimination of great suffering through a
            little suffering   372
          2″ Though there is a little suffering in the
            deeds of the Mahāyāna, it is unsuitable to
            despise that which completely eliminates
            suffering   373–4
          3″ Rightness of making effort for the sake of
            great bliss; wrongness of being attached
            to small pleasures   375–7
          4″ Suitability of liking the Mahāyāna   378
          5″ Summation   379
       2′ Proving that the Mahāyāna scriptures are the word
        of Buddha   380–9
        a′ The deeds of the six perfections   380–2
          1″ Not the slightest bad explanation in the
            scriptures of the Mahāyāna   380
          2″ The aims of the Mahāyāna are taught
            in the Mahāyāna scriptures   381
          3″ Therefore, those scriptures are proved
            to be the word of Buddha   382
        b′ Necessity of knowing the complete path of
         the great enlightenment from the scriptures
         of the Mahāyāna   383
        c′ Necessity of knowing the great nature of a

STANZA

Buddha from the Mahāyāna which therefore
is the word of Buddha   384–9
   1″ Limitless causes of the Body of Form
     are explained in the Mahāyāna   384–5
   2″ Knowledge of extinction explained in the
     Hīnayāna and extinction and no
     production explained in the Mahāyāna
     have the same meaning of the cognition
     of emptiness   386–7
   3″ If the meaning of the Mahāyāna is not
     understood, it is right to be indifferent
     toward it but not to despise it   388–9
  3′ Incompleteness of the paths and fruits of the
   Mahāyāna as explained in the Hīnayāna
   scriptures   390–3
   a′ The deeds of Bodhisattvas are not completely
     explained in the Hīnayāna scriptures   390–1
   b′ Buddhahood cannot be achieved through
     practising just the four noble truths and
     the auxiliaries to enlightenment   392
   c′ The Mahāyāna scriptures are suitable to be
     considered by the wise as the word of Buddha   393
  4′ Purpose of teaching three vehicles   394–6
  (b) Summation   397–8
3 Summation   399
4 Advice to become a monk if unable to learn the special
royal ways   400

Chapter Five: Advice for even Bodhisattvas wishing quickly to
attain liberation to become monks   401–87

1 Brief teachings of what is to be adopted and discarded by
Bodhisattva householders and monks   401–2
2 Extensive exposition   403–87
  a Forsaking defects   403–34b
  (1) Extensive explanation of the fifty-seven defects to be
   forsaken   403–33
   (a) The first fifteen, anger, etc.   403–12
    1′ The fourteen, anger, etc.   403–6b

		STANZA
2' Pride		406c–12
(b) From hypocrisy to the forty-first, not thinking of death		413–25
(c) The forty-second, proclaiming one's own virtues, etc.		426–33
(2) Summation		434ab
b Adopting virtues		434c–87
(1) Temporary virtues		434c–61b
(a) General teaching		434c–9
1' Brief description of the entities of virtues		434c–5
2' Identifying their individual entities		436–7
3' Individual effects		438
4' General effect		439
(b) Qualities of the ten stages		440–61b
1' Just as there are eight levels of Hearers, so there are ten Bodhisattva stages		440
2' Entities and qualities of the ten stages		441–60
3' Summation		461ab
(2) Final virtues		461c–87
(a) Each of a Buddha's virtues is limitless		461c–3
1' The Buddhas' limitless virtues depend on the ten powers		461c–62b
2' Examples of the limitlessness of Buddhas' virtues		462c–3
(b) Causes for generating belief and faith in the limitless virtues of Buddhas		464–87
1' The reason why the Buddhas' virtues are limitless is that the merits which are their causes are limitless		464–8
a' Source for the limitlessness of the Buddhas' virtues		464
b' Way to amass limitless merit		465
c' Brief presentation of the seven branches		466–8
2' Limitlessness of the causes because of aspiring to help limitless beings		469–85
3' Immeasurability of the merit of those virtues		486
4' Sources		487
III Conclusion		488–500
A Advice to generate inspiration for the practices and to observe the four practices		488–90

		STANZA
B	Faults of not relying on a teacher and qualifications of a teacher	491–3ab
C	The supreme fruit is achieved through excellent behaviour	493c–7
1	Achieving the supreme fruit	493cd
2	Advice to perform the special deeds	494–7
a	Extensive mode of behaviour	494–5
b	Condensed mode of behaviour	496
c	Very condensed mode of behaviour	497
D	These doctrines are not just for kings but also for all others	498
E	Exhorting the king to heed the advice	499–500
1	Suitability of continuously thinking of the welfare of others	499
2	Suitability of adopting virtues	500

Notes

1 The fruits previously described were effects within a human life which accord with the causes. Here, concordant effects as entire lifetimes in bad migrations are indicated.

2 'In fact' means 'ultimately' or 'as existing able to bear analysis'.

3 The surviving Sanskrit text is a little different here as in verses 47, 49, 51, 102, 123, 130, 138, 142, 342, etc. However, the Tibetan texts are followed because the translations into Tibetan were compared with three Sanskrit texts.

4 The production of suffering is caused by the conception of inherent existence, its cessation is caused by the path.

5 Previous to and simultaneously with their effects.

5a The Sanskrit has another interpretation which is offered by the other Tibetan edition: 'When there is no tall, / Short does not exist through its own nature, / Just as due to the non-production of a flame, / Light also does not arise.'

6 The followers of Kanāḍa, i.e., the Vaiśeṣikas.

7 Sanskrit for the last two lines: 'How could the produced, the stayed / And the ceased exist in fact?'

8 It is not seen that only a part of a thing changes. Also, if an atom changed completely, it could not be said, as the Vaiśeṣikas do, that it is permanent but its states are impermanent.

9 'Baseless' means not providing a base for the conception that things inherently exist.

10 'Forders' are, in Sanskrit, *Tīrthika*, i.e., non-Buddhists who propound and follow a path or ford to liberation or high status.

11 The aggregates and the self are not inexpressible as either one or different because all phenomena are either one or different.

12 Water, fire and wind; or cohesion, heat and motility.

13 The potencies of the four elements are said to be present in everything; the predominance of one element over the others determines what is manifested.

14 The constituents are earth, water, fire, wind, space and consciousness which are imputed to be a self.

15 See note 14.

16 It has already been established that there are no inherently existent things and no inherently existing trueness; thus, there are no inherently existent non-things or inherently existent falseness, because the latter exist only in relation to the former.

17 An objector wonders, 'Innumerable Buddhas are effecting the liberation of even more sentient beings; there are no new sentient beings; thus in time all would be liberated. Since of course such extinguishing or liberating of worldly beings does not increase the number of beings, the world must eventually have an end. Thus, why did Buddha remain silent about an end to the world?

18 The first extreme of the world's having limits is propounded by the Nihilists who say that the self is finished in this life and does not go on to a future life. The second extreme of the world's not having limits is propounded by the Sāṃkhyas who say that the self of this life goes to the next life. The third extreme of the world's both having and not having limits is propounded by the Jainas who say that the states of the self have limits but the nature of the self has no limits. The fourth extreme of the world's neither having nor not having limits is propounded by the Buddhist Proponents of a Self (Pudgalavādin) who say that there is a real self which is utterly unpredictable as permanent or impermanent.

19 Those who accept emptiness but take it to mean nothingness.

20 Those who take emptiness to mean a denial of cause and effect and therefore reject emptiness.

21 'Speaking pleasantly' is conversation based on high status and definite goodness. 'Behaving with purpose' is causing others to practise what is helpful. 'Concordance' is for one to practise what one teaches others.

22 Sometimes a horrible effect of a bad deed is seen in this life and sometimes it is not seen until the next life. If comfort is taken because the effects are not seen, why is fear of those actions not generated when the effects are seen?

23 The nine orifices are eyes, ears, nose, mouth, genitals and anus.

24 Reliquaries here are actual Buddhas.

24a This is a round, fleshy swelling on the crown or top of a Buddha's head; it is perceptible but its size is not.

25 A circle of hairs between the brows.

26 The chapter has an extra verse and Gyel-tsap (rGyal-tshab) does not comment on this verse which also has an extra line; therefore, it is set off in brackets.

27 This pain is a special form of virtue, and the word does not imply that it is unwanted.

28 The last line follows an alternative reading given by Gyel-tsap. Otherwise, it is, 'And respectfully rely on them with the six practices.'

29 Tīrthika.

30 Spells for relieving illness and the names and purposes of medicines are to be posted.

31 Sugar, ghee, honey, sesame oil and salt.

32 The skill of reducing many emanations to one and vice versa, etc.

33 Building temples and enduring difficulties for the sake of the doctrine.

34 The Tibetan translation offers two meanings for the last Sanskrit line, the first using *yasmāt* and the second *tasmāt*.

35 'Great exaltation' refers to the wide scope of his temple building and other public services.

36 Tibetan omits 'clothing'.

37 The objects apprehended by the other senses cannot be known to be pleasurable because the thought of pleasure can pay attention only to one object at a time.

38 The present must depend on the past and the future in order to be present, but if the present does not exist in the past and future, then it cannot truly depend on them. If the present does exist in the past and the future, then it is not different from them.

39 If the four elements were completely intermingled, they would lose their individual characters.

40 Is there a mind which certifies the existence of a mind cognising reality? If there were a second mind perceiving the first mind and existing simultaneously, it could certify the true existence of the first; however, all minds depend on mental factors and are thus unreal; also the certifier would need a certifier. Thus, only conventionally is it said that the mind sees reality.

41 The inequality would be to consider one as the word of Buddha and one as not.

42 If due to the complexity of Buddha's teaching one cannot understand it, indifference or neutrality is best.

43 Forms, sounds odours, tastes and tangible objects.

44 Viewing the mental and physical aggregates which are a transitory collection as a real self, afflicted doubt and considering bad ethics and disciplines to be superior.

45 Yāma.

46 Tuṣita.

47 Nirmāṇarati.

48 Paranirmitavaśavartin.

49 This is translated in accordance with Nāgārjuna's views as set forth in his works on the Highest Yoga Tantra (Anuttarayogatantra).

II

The Song of the Four Mindfulnesses Causing the Rain of Achievements to Fall

Instructions for Meditation on the View of Emptiness

KAYSANG GYATSO
The Seventh Dalai Lama

Introduction

The second work in this volume is a short poem that contains within it the essentials of sūtra and tantra:

1 The admiration for one who teaches the path to enlightenment.
2 The thought definitely to leave cyclic existence and the consequent wish to attain highest enlightenment in order to help all sentient beings.
3 The simultaneous and swift collection of merit and wisdom through imagining oneself as a deity who is qualified by emptiness.
4 The realisation of emptiness which is coupled with its application to the world of appearances.

For the sake of easy memorisation and subsequent application in meditation the Seventh Dalai Lama (1708–57) versified these concise teachings, which were originally given by Mañjuśrī to Tsong-ka-pa. The translation is based on oral transmissions and explanations of the text received from His Holiness Tenzin Gyatso, the Fourteenth Dalai Lama, in Dharamsala, India, in May and August of 1972.

Instructions for Meditation on the View of Emptiness, The Song of the Four Mindfulnesses, Causing the Rain of Achievements to Fall

1 Mindfulness of the Teacher

On the seat of the immutable union of method and wisdom
Sits the kind teacher who is the entity of all the refuges,
A Buddha who has perfect abandonment and wisdom is there.
Forsaking thoughts of defects, make a petition with pure perception,
Not letting your mind stray, place it within admiration and respect,
Making your attention unforgetful, maintain it within admiration and respect.

2 Mindfulness of the Altruistic Aspiration to Highest Enlightenment

In the prison of the suffering of limitless cyclic existence
Wander the six types of sentient beings[1] bereft of happiness,
Fathers and mothers who protected you with kindness are there.
Forsaking desire and hatred, meditate on endearment and compassion,
Not letting your mind stray, place it within compassion,
Making your attention unforgetful, maintain it within compassion.

3 Mindfulness of Your Body as a Divine Body

In the divine mansion of great bliss, pleasant to feel,
Abides the divine body which is your own body of pure aggregates and constituents,
A deity with the Three Bodies[2] inseparable is there.
Not conceiving yourself to be ordinary, practise divine pride and vivid appearance,

Not letting your mind stray, place it within the profound and the manifest[3]

Making your attention unforgetful, maintain it within the profound and the manifest.

4   *Mindfulness of the View of Emptiness*

Throughout the circle of appearing and occurring objects of knowledge

Pervades the space of clear light which is reality, the ultimate,

An inexpressible mode of being of objects is there.

Forsaking mental fabrications,[4] *look to the entity of immaculate emptiness*

Not letting your mind stray, place it within reality,

Making your attention unforgetful, maintain it within reality.

At the cross-roads of the varieties of appearances and the six consciousnesses

Is seen the confusion of the baseless phenomena of duality,

The illusory spectacles of a deceiving magician are there.

Not thinking they are true, look to their entity of emptiness,

Not letting your mind stray, place it within appearance and emptiness,

Making your attention unforgetful, maintain it within appearance and emptiness.

These instructions on the view of emptiness for one who uses the four mindfulnesses, which are special precepts actually bestowed by the holy Mañjughoṣa on Tsong-ka-pa, a king of doctrine, were composed by the Buddhist monk Losang Kaysang Gyatso (bLo-bzang-bskal-bzang-rgya-mtsho) for the sake of his own and others' establishing predispositions for the correct view.

Notes

1 Gods, demigods, humans, animals, hungry ghosts, and denizens of hells.
2 Body of Truth or wisdom consciousness, Body of Enjoyment or spontaneous speech, and Body of Form or physical body.
3 Profound emptiness and manifest appearance.
4 Mental fabrications which posit an object negated by emptiness other than inherent existence.